23
10
10

40 (50)

1

Table of Contents

Introduction to the Certified Accounting Management (CMA) Test

The CMA examination is specifically designed by committees of the world's top leading management accounting professionals to test advanced skills in management accounting. The CMA designation demonstrates your ability to perform masterful financial planning, analysis, decision support and control. There are many requirements to obtain and keep the CMA designation. However, the value the designation gives a working professional has significant return on investment. The average CMA designee gets paid, on average, $34,000 more per year than the average noncertified peer according to IMA Annual Salary Survey, Strategic Finance, June 2013. Yet the entire testing process can cost as little as $2,500!

The CMA exam has two parts, with each section focused on a specific area as shown below:

Part 1: Financial Analysis, Performance and Control

- Planning, budgeting and forecasting
- Performance measurement
- Cost management
- Internal controls
- Professional ethics

Part 2: Financial Decisions

- Financial statement analysis
- Corporate finance
- Decision analysis and risk management
- Investment decisions
- Professional ethics

Through the rest of this document, you will find the resources necessary to get you started on your journey to acquire the CMA designation. This is not a complete resource and one does not exist – the marketplace fluctuates far too much for any one resource to ever capture all of its aspects, let alone management accounting specifically. However, if you study this book well, you will succeed on the CMA test.

Enjoy your study time and the journey you are beginning by starting the process of becoming a Certified Management Accountant!

Educational Requirement

All CMA candidates must have a Bachelor's Degree from an accredited college or university. An official English transcript must be submitted with the official seal of the college or university. Any degrees from a non-accredited institution must be evaluated.

Professional Experience Requirement

The required professional experience is to complete two full time continuous years in management accounting and/or financial management. This experience can be completed before taking the exam or with seven years of passing the CMA test. Part time employment can be applied as long as it is at least 20 hours per week for four years.

Note that the above positions require using management accounting principles as a requirement of the position. Positions such as sales and marketing, engineering, computer operations, personnel, or general management as well as non-technical, clerical or internships do *not* satisfy this requirement.

Registration and Scheduling

CMA tests are computerized, and are administered at facilities all around the world. This gives an applicant some flexibility in testing location. There are three testing timeframes: January/February, May/June and September/October. Keep these timeframes in mind for when you file your Exam Registration Form because the registration numbers you receive have an expiration date. Here are the first steps you must take in order to take the CMA test:

1. File an Exam Registration Form selecting which exams you plan to take

2. Pay the applicable fees.

3. Receive a Registration Acknowledgement Form containing your authorization numbers, your testing windows and the "Instructions for Candidates" booklet.

4. Go online and schedule the actual test at the location that works best for you in your allotted timeframe.

5. Show up to your scheduled exam early and be prepared to give required identification. Check with your local testing facility as to what documentation is required.

Do note that the exam is given in two parts and you only have to take one part during an exam window. However, you only have three years to complete both parts or your passing credit will expire. The three-year window begins the date of your Registration Acknowledgement Form. If the passing credit expires, you will have to retake that part again and pay the retake fees.

Test Parameters to Expect

Each part of the CMA test consists of 100 multiple-choice questions and you have three hours to complete it. The multiple-choice questions have four options with only one correct answer. Less than 50% correct on these sections will stop you from moving onto the essay sections. The essay sections contain 8 to 10 calculation or response questions based on two scenarios involving a typical business situation which you must answer within one hour.

According to the Institute of Certified Management Accountants, the skills that will be tested on the exam are defined as follows:

- *Knowledge*: Ability to remember previously learned material such as specific facts, criteria, techniques, principles, and procedures (i.e., identify, define, list).

- *Comprehension*: Ability to grasp and interpret the meaning of material (i.e., classify, explain, distinguish between).

- *Application*: Ability to use learned material in new and concrete situations (i.e., demonstrate, predict, solve, modify, relate).

- *Analysis*: Ability to break down material in to its component parts so that its organizational structure can be understood; ability to recognize causal relationships, discriminate between behaviors, and identify elements that are relevant to the validation of a judgment (i.e., differentiate, estimate, order).

- *Synthesis*: Ability to put parts together to form a new whole or proposed set of operations; ability to relate ideas and formulate hypotheses (i.e. combine, formulate, revise).

- *Evaluation*: Ability to judge the value of material for a given purpose on the basis of consistency, logical accuracy, and comparison to standards; ability to appraise judgments involved in the selection of a course of action (i.e., criticize, justify, conclude).

Given that the CMA test is meant to prove your mastery of the management accounting skills, the test will include all the above skill levels with an emphasis on the highest level, which is Evaluation.

Before jumping straight in to the specific testing topics of the CMA exam, there are some primary assumptions and general understandings that need to be clarified between financial accounting and management accounting.

According to the National Association of Accountants (NAA), Management Accounting is the process of identification, measurement, accumulation, analysis, preparation, interpretation and communication of financial information, which is used by management to plan, evaluate, and control within an organization and to insure that a company's resources are used and accounted for appropriately.

Management accounting is an internal company process that doesn't have to comply with external laws and regulations about financial data analysis specifically because it is internal. Financial accounting must adhere to Generally Accepted Accounting Practices (GAAP) as well as all tax laws/legislation on all judiciary levels and all Securities Exchange Commission (SEC) regulations because it must report financial data to external entities outside of the company. This simple difference leaves management accounting a very broad field to master across a single large company, let alone when you look at a specific industry, yet the CMA exam is to prove your mastery of management accounting across the entire global market.

Given you meet the educational requirement to even consider taking the CMA exam, you clearly have the mathematical skills necessary. If there are specific areas you struggle with, such as the math or accounting techniques necessary to complete a problem in the multiple-choice questions at the end of this guide, there are plenty of other focused resources at your disposal to get the support you need. Therefore, this study guide will focus on the practical concepts and methodologies that make up management accounting. This guide is focused on hitting as many of the main topic points on the test as possible, from basics to advanced topics, without going into too much depth. You should have a strong handle on the basics if you are challenging the CMA test – if you need help with specific accounting principles outside the purview of this test, you would be wise to seek out further resources.

Part 1: Financial Planning, Performance and Control

Planning, Budgeting and Forecasting

Budgets are the primary instrument for planning and forecasting within an organization. The role of budgets within an organization have many diverse layers. A budget's primary purpose is to set clear expectations from management as to all financial transactions for a given time period. Once actuals are accumulated, the budget then plays a pivotal role in creating specific performance measures. From evaluation of these specific measures in performance, a new budget is planned with any adjustments needed contributing to forecasts.

Let's go over some budget basics. The master budget is classified broadly into two categories: the operational budget and the financial budget. The operational budget reflects the results of operating decision while the financial budget reflects the financial decisions of a company. The operating budget consists of:

1. Sales budget including a computation of expected earnings
2. Production budget
3. Ending inventory budget
4. Direct material budget including a computation of expected cost disbursements for materials
5. Direct labor budget
6. Factory overhead budget
7. Sales and administration budget
8. Pro forma statement.

The financial budget consists of the cash budget and the pro forma balance sheet. The major steps for preparing the budget are:

1. Prepare a sales forecast
2. Determine production volume
3. Estimate manufacturing costs and operating expenses
4. Determine cash flow and other financial effects
5. Formulate projected financial statements.

The one data center that begins the master budget process is the sales budget. It is the only budget created entirely from estimated customer demand for a given time period. From the sales budget, resources are allocated to varying departments to handle the demand. This budget affects other department budgets for direct materials, direct labor, overhead, etc. All the other budgets give feedback to top management on what is needed overall for the company development of annual profits.

A primary source for the sales budget is the sales forecast. To create a sales forecast, executives must take account of external factors such as local and national economies, the industry economy and the market competition with their sales volume and pricing. They must also account for internal factors such as number of units sold in prior periods, company credit policies, company collection policies, company pricing policies, new products being brought to market by the company and the company's facility manufacturing capacity. All of this is incorporated in to the sales forecast and then pulled in to the sales budget.

The sales budget directly affects the production budget. Items must be produced before they can be sold and no company wants inventory just sitting on shelves not moving. So if the sales budget over forecasts demand too much, a company is left with a warehouse full of goods that has no real demand and a lot of money spent likely without recouping enough money to cover the full production costs within that time period. However, if the sales budget under forecasts too much, the warehouse is empty but labor costs will increase in an attempt to keep up with the unforeseen demand. Parts may end up on back order and the company has unhappy customers waiting for products. The more accurate the sales budget, the more the production budget can maintain efficiency and handle customer demand.

The production budget informs the company of how many units of what products can be produced while having to manage all inventory. This includes completed products as well as maintaining all parts for the products and depending on the level of manufacturing includes keeping all replaceable machine parts on hand to maintain the equipment operating efficiency. These varying inventory levels are constantly in flux and all parts are on different timeframes. If some parts come from China to the United States, those parts could take anywhere from 8 to 10 weeks to arrive at the facility so these clearly need to be managed with that extended timeframe for delivery in mind, while other parts may come from a neighboring state that can be sent overnight if demand changes quickly. While the company needs these parts, once parts are purchased the funds are now tied up and cannot be used for anything else until that part is used to complete the product and be sold. Other inventory to be managed are common items used on the production floor, such as if the production floor simply uses a big drum of oil to use on moving parts. This is a typical inventory item missed in the general count but once the floor runs out of oil, production stops! This can obviously have huge consequences for an entire production department. These fluctuating inventory levels require a high level of tracking and reporting such that the production manager can create the production budget accurately according to the sales budget and sales forecast.

The ending inventory budget provides the information needed to construct budgeted financial statements. This is beneficial for calculating the cost of goods sold on the budgeted income statement while it gives the dollar value of the ending materials and the finished goods inventory that will appear on the budgeted balance sheet.

The production budget and the ending inventory budget leads to the direct materials budget and direct labor budget by stating how many units the production department has to make to meet the sales budget. This then equates to the direct materials budget for inventory on hand and items to be purchased with any additional costs associated with the materials purchased, such as shipping or interest rate charges for items purchased with credit. Policy is very important in regards to the direct materials budget because of the extra costs that can creep up on the company. Clear policies as to what percentage levels of inventory should be kept on hand as well as purchasing and procurement practices that the company approves of can significantly mitigate direct materials creep. The direct labor budget is used in determining how many employees are needed in what periods for optimal production output. The direct labor budget also lets managers know if they need to hire more workers or reduce the labor force.

The factory overhead budget then takes all the information from the production budget and creates a detailed plan of material production costs other than direct materials and direct labor that are needed to meet budgeted production needs. This information has two purposes. One purpose is to integrate the overhead cost budgets of the production department and related departments. The other purpose is to group the information for calculation of future overhead accounting periods.

The next budget to discuss is the sales and administrative budget. This is a detailed plan of expenses required for operations that are not tied to production. These are period costs that the accountants use to estimate cash payments for products or services not used in production-related activities. This budget can have a large impact on the contribution margin of a company if costs are not kept under control. All sales and administrative expenses, as well as cost of goods sold, are subtracted from sales to create the contribution margin. If a company gets carried away with spending too much money on office parties and meetings, this directly affects the contribution margin in a negative way by overhead placing too much burden on the company's income. If a company keeps overhead costs low yet can still efficiently run the company at optimal efficiency, the company will have more profits to grow and expand.

The cash budget is the overall intake and outflow of cash for an organization, so this budget is prepared in order to forecast a company's future needs. It is also a tool for cash planning and control. The cash budget typically has four sections:

1. A receipts section with the beginning cash balance, cash collections from customers and other receipts
2. A disbursements section will show all cash payments made and listed by purpose
3. A cash surplus or deficit section will show the difference between the cash receipts and the cash disbursements sections
4. A financing section will provide a detailed account of the borrowings and repayments expected during the budget period.

These cash budgets are used as supporting documents for a Pro Forma statement. Pro Forma statements are used as financial projections in business and expansion plans to external parties, usually to raise funds. On a side note, capital expenditure budgets give a detailed outline of anticipated amounts and timing of capital outlays for long-term assets during an accounting period.

The relationships between economic conditions and industry conditions to a company's plans and budgets are significant. A well-stewarded company will be aware of economic conditions and the way those affect their industry. Incorporating the economic and industry conditions in to a company's plans and budgets should act as a basis or foundation for the company to move forward. Most people get the concept that a budget is a road map for the company. The economic and industry conditions give clues as to the type of terrain the map or budget has to lead the company through.

With financial budgets in place, operational objectives can be created and measured for performance. These short-term objectives are stepping stones to make sure structures and systems are in place for the intended financial decisions set out by the budgets. These short-term structures act as controls to ensure that the company is in the proper position to fulfill on the next objective. Back to the map analogy, the current short-term objective may be to continue straight ahead, but if you are not aware that you need to make a left turn up ahead you can end up in the wrong lane and setting your organization up for a wild ride of over-correcting to attempt to get back on track.

Budgets originate from the company's created goals or targets. The budgets are in place to act as a way to control internal decisions for a given period, and then act as a comparison with the actual transactions in that same given time period. This allows for measuring the performance of an organization towards established goals. The budget is the theorized future as seen by the company. When compared to the actuals, the budget allows management to see how accurate their theorized future was. This allows the management team to learn and develop the next budget with greater accuracy.

The definition of successful budgeting processes can fluctuate according to the goal of the budget. However, there are some basic characteristics for successful budgeting processes:

- Clear objectives and goals set before the budget is created
- Accurate data as to what resources exist within the organization that can be incorporated in to the budget
- Clear measurement standards for evaluating the budget verses actuals
- Clear and accepted chains of command and accountability
- Open lines of communication so that budget analysis can be used across all departments to support future growth and stability

The budgeting process should include accurate data from all departments. This requires open lines of communication in both directions within the organization. As long as departments are acknowledged for what they contribute to the company and as long as the budgeting department realizes that it is a part of the organization, the company as a whole can coordinate efforts more efficiently to obtain large organizational goals and objectives while developing the company as a whole, organic unit.

One of the primary tools a manager has in affecting their department's budget and performance evaluation is how they handle their controllable costs. A controllable cost is when a department head or manager is assigned responsibility for the cost and has direct and significant influence on the amount of the cost. In other words, all variable costs, variable overhead, direct materials and direct labor are all examples of controllable costs a manager may have at their disposal. If a manager handles direct labor more efficiently to minimize labor costs while maintaining a high level of production, the manager is likely to get good departmental and performance reviews.

When managers have a good grasp on operations in their departments, they can give more accurate feedback to the top management as to the resources available for the company as a whole for budgeting purposes. For instance, if the manager from the previous paragraph has accomplished such a high level of efficiency that his department can now take on more projects, this creates more direct labor resources for the company to evaluate the best use for this resource. If other departments are not ready for this next level of production, new objectives will be created in an attempt to bring all the other departments to a new level of production. If these objectives are met, then the company as a whole can produce more and in turn create more profit for further growth. However, if that manager never clearly reported the increase in productivity, the budgeting department would likely not know what areas it would be best to develop first to take the company to the next level. The importance of accurate data collection for a company's resources can have a very direct and significant effect on the company's future growth or failure.

Determining who should be a direct part of the budgeting process can be difficult because managerial time is an important resource. Companies should include evaluating the efficiency of their budgeting meetings when evaluating their company resources. All aspects of the company need to be represented in the budgets; however, manager representation of all departments during the budget creation process may not be necessary if proper lines of communication are in place. With smaller companies, it may work to have all managers as part of the budget creation process due to the nature of managers in these companies wearing multiple job titles and having cross-functioning duties. Larger companies need to keep a watchful eye on overhead, which is influenced by the efficiency of their managers.

Cost standards are another tool companies can use to evaluate the performance for any given department. Careful determination and understanding of cost standards assist in creating the targeted goal for production costs, which leads to accurate budgeting. Comparing the actual costs to the standard costs can give insight into many different levels of performance for cost departments while assisting the budget creation process to create more accurate cost predictions.

Sometimes companies get carried away with ideas for a company and their standards become more theoretical than practical. Having ideals to strive for can be a good thing to create positive momentum and inspiration within a company as long as the company distinguishes that they are ideals. Practical standards are necessary for accurate evaluation purposes and to avoid burnout for employees. Companies need a balance of practical standards and ideals to grow towards in order to keep the company in a forward-looking frame of mind for continued growth.

There is a difference between authoritative verses and participative standards. Authoritative standards are handed directly down throughout an organization. They are generally clear directions for what departments need to do, but with no direct feedback to top management about the standards. This can lead to targets that may be unrealistic and unattainable while seriously damaging motivation throughout the entire organization. Participative standards in budgeting is a process where personnel at all levels in the organization actively engage in the budget decisions of a company. This is the key to successful company budgeting!

Top management needs feedback in order create company policy regarding budgets that accommodate for the impact of significant changes in budget assumptions. A company should evaluate in what kind of situations the current budget should be revised instead of just reflecting changes in next year's budget. What type of market conditions should call for the budget committee to meet about the impact on the company? These type of triggering events need to be reviewed and discussed for each budgeting year. The economy seems to keep moving faster and faster, so the only way for companies to keep up is to be prepared to quickly change course.

With budgeting now discussed in length, let's move on to forecasting. Simple regression forecasting is, for example, forecasting overhead costs based only on one data source, such as on machine hours. This can be useful in acquiring a quick estimate or to give a general cross reference checkpoint on a more in-depth analysis.

Multiple regression analysis is a statistical forecasting method involving several different data points, such as machine hours and labor hours, to reach forecasting conclusions. This analysis involves financial calculus and needs accurate data. Multiple regression analysis is primarily used when a company wants to look at the mathematical relationship between action activities and costs. For instance, 70% of the total variation of factory overhead might be explained by the regression equation or the change in machine hours, and the remaining 30% might be accounted for by something other than machine hours.

Another important tool to remember is the learning curve analysis when it comes to labor hour forecasting. This analysis is based on the proposition that labor hours decrease in a definite pattern as labor operations are repeated. Essentially, it is based on statistical data: As the cumulative output doubles, the average cumulative labor input time required per unit will be reduced by some constrained percentage. This number is usually somewhere between 10% and 40%. For example, if the rate of reduction is 10% the curve is referred to as a 90% learning curve.

Policies are very important when it comes to the cash budget. Company policies for how to obtain credit and how to treat payables allows for clear decisions for when and what to purchase in a given accounting period, which in turn helps to control the cash budget through all levels of purchasing decisions in an organization.

Performance measurement is the use of quantitative tools to gauge an organization's performance in relation to an expected outcome or specific goal. Typically, these expected outcomes are created from a standard costing system. Standard costing systems are a methodology of cost control that includes a measure of actual performance and a measure of variance between standard and actual performance. The variances provide measures of performance used to assist managers to control costs. Operations and managerial performance can also be communicated by use of standard cost reports.

A responsibility center is an organizational unit whose manager has the responsibility of managing a portion of the organization's resources. There are five different types of responsibility centers:

- Investment center – the manager of this center is accountable for profit generation and making significant decisions about the resources the center uses.
- Profit center – the manager of this center is accountable for revenue and costs, as well as the resulting operating income.
- Revenue center – the manager of this center is primarily accountable for revenue; this manager's success is primarily based on their ability to generate income.
- Discretionary cost center – the manager of this center accountable for costs only when the relationship between company resources and the production of products/services is not well-defined.
- Cost center the manager of this center is accountable only for controllable costs that have well-defined relationships between the center's resources and certain products or services.

There is a lot of accountability tied up within responsibility centers. Thus, the allocation of common costs among segments causes problems in performance evaluation, because how can a manager be accountable for a center variance when they have no direct control over the cost to their center? These type of issues need to be addressed through company policy and foresight in to future evaluation standards.

When a large company has multiple divisions and centers, at some point there will be a need to exchange products or services between divisions and centers but if the company has performance measurements in place, how does this work? Transfer pricing is the price a company chooses to use in this situation. Transfer prices are never used externally and simply allow the transaction to be measured and accounted for within the company. This affects the revenue and costs of the divisions but not the company revenue and costs as a whole. There are three basic kinds of transfer prices:

- Cost-Plus transfer prices, which are based on either the variable costs incurred or the full costs incurred by the producing division, plus an agreed-upon profit percentage. The downside of using cost-plus transfer prices is that cost recovery is guaranteed to the selling division, which prevents the company from discovering inefficient operation conditions, creating excessive costs that may reward ill-performing departments and lead to an overall reduction in profitability or shareholder value.

- Market transfer prices, which are based on the current market value of the product or service. These keep the selling department from raising the price for an internal buyer. However, this can lead to a reduction in the selling department's willingness to sell internally, because they can't negotiate. Profits may suffer if this leads to an internal shortage of materials and causes other departments to purchase outside of the company.

- Negotiated transfer prices, which are between the negotiation floor (the selling division's cost price) and the negotiation ceiling (the market price.) This allows for cost recovery while still allowing the selling division to maintain profitability.

With profit being such an important topic for companies and a primary performance measure, let's discuss return on investment (ROI). ROI is operating income divided by assets invested, where assets invested is the average of the beginning and ending asset balances for the period. Proper measurement of income and assets specifically controlled by a manager is critical to the quality of this performance measure. Many factors affect ROI, and this can lead some managers to placing their department's ROI above the company's overall profits or other resource center's sustainability. So ROI as a performance measure should always be used in conjunction with other measures, such as residual income (RI). RI is the operating income that an investment center earns above a desired return on invested assets. RI is not a ratio but a dollar amount, the dollar amount of profit left after subtracting a predetermined desired income target for an investment center. The desired RI will vary from investment center to investment center depending on the type of business and risk level assumed. Care must be taken when comparing investment centers within a company. The RI figures need to be comparable with all investment centers having equal access to resources and similar asset investment bases. Otherwise, this can lead to the appearance of some managers performing better than others when they simply have a larger pool of assets to draw from. So both ROI and RI have some flaws independently and this is why companies need multiple performance measures for all their resource centers.

A primary tool to balance all the different performance measures, a company's vision and mission, strategic and tactical plans, resources along with linking the perspectives of an organization's four basic stakeholder groups – financial (investors), learning and growth (employees), internal business processes and customers – is the balanced scorecard. An organization must add value to all stakeholder groups in order to succeed in both the short term and long term. A company will determine each group's objectives and translates them in to performance measures that have specific, quantifiable targets and keep track of them all in a broad sense with the balanced scorecard.

Performance measures are incredibly complex and need to be created with future adjustments in mind at all levels, from policy creation to how customers receive quality products. Given the complexities of performance measures, this is an incredibly difficult area to create structures and at the same time very easy for small mistakes in calculations to have huge negative impacts for an entire organization.

When it comes to cost management, the most important thing to be clear on is the difference between fixed and variable costs in the long term and short term, and how changes in assumptions regarding cost type or relevant range affect these costs. A fixed cost is a cost that remains constant within a defined range of activity or time period. A variable cost is one that changes in direct proportion to a change in productive output (or some other measure of volume). Some fixed costs become variable over a greater period of time such as insurance rates and property taxes, or if there is a building expansion that creates a significant change to what the fixed price was prior to expansion as an example of how relevant range can affect costs. Shifting a cost from overhead to, for example, cost of goods sold can also affect whether the cost is fixed or variable. Having clear structures as to how to classify costs through the organization is imperative in having accurate financials for the company to make good decisions. These structures are the cost allocation. Cost allocation is putting structures in place for assigning a collection of indirect objects to a specific cost object like a product or service, a department, or an operating activity using an allocation base called a cost driver. A cost driver might be direct labor or any other activity base that has a cause-and-effect relationship with the cost. The cost pool is a collection of indirect costs assigned to a cost object.

Another primary topic to remember in cost management is that materials inventory and work-in-progress inventory support the production process, while finished goods inventory supports the sales and distribution functions of an organization. The cost of direct materials purchased increases the balance of the materials inventory account while the cost of direct materials used by the production department decreases it. The work-in-progress inventory account records the balance of partially completed units of production. As direct labor and direct materials enter the production process, their costs add to the work-in-progress inventory account. The total costs of direct labor, direct materials and overhead costs incurred and transferred to work-in-progress inventory during an accounting period is called current manufacturing costs or total manufacturing costs. The cost of all units completed and moved to finished goods inventory during an accounting process is called the cost of goods manufactured. The cost of goods manufactured for the period decreases the balance of the work-in-progress inventory account. The finished goods inventory account holds the balance of costs assigned to all completed products that a manufacturing company has not sold. The cost of goods manufactured increases the balance while the costs of goods sold decreases the balance.

Cost management techniques are a foundational basic that any manager needs to understand. The actual costing method uses the costs of direct labor, direct materials and overhead at the end of an accounting period, or when actual costs become known, to calculate the unit product cost. The actual product unit cost is assigned to the finished goods inventory on the balance sheet and to the costs of goods sold on the income statement. The normal costing technique combines the actual direct costs with estimated overhead costs to determine a product unit cost. At the end of the accounting period, any difference between the estimated and actual costs must be identified and removed such that the financial statements show only the actual costs. When product costs must be estimated beforehand, the standard costing method can be useful, such as to price a proposed product for a customer. This method uses estimated or standard costs of direct cost plus overhead to calculate the product unit cost.

Variable costing is a method of preparing profit center performance reports that classifies a manager's controllable costs as either variable or fixed. Variable costing produces a variable costing income statement instead of a traditional income statement, also known as absorption costing income statement, which is used for external reporting purposes. Variable costing affects the value of inventory, costs of goods sold and operating income by only including variable costs for manufacturing meaning only direct labor, direct materials and variable overhead costs are used to compute variable costs of goods sold. Understanding the affects variable costing has on the bottom line is imperative.

A decision about whether to sell a joint product at the split-off point or sell it after further processing is called a sell or process-further decision. A joint product is two or more products made from the same material or process that cannot be identified as separate products or services during all or some of the processing. Only at the split-off point do joint products or services become separate and identifiable. At that point, a company can choose to sell the product or service as it is, or process it in to another form of sale for market. Some joint products are called byproducts because their sale value is minor in comparison to the other joint products. Costs incurred after the split-off point are called separable costs.

There are multiple accumulation costing systems. They are job order costing, process costing and activity-based costing. Job order costing is where costs are associated by jobs. With process costing, the costs are traced to production processes. Activity-based costing (ABC) is used to assign activity costs to cost objects. Each system has benefits and

Theory of Constraints
Value Chain
Outsourcing
Just-in-time manufacturing

When it comes to internal controls, a company's organizational structure, policies, objectives, goals, management philosophy and management style influence the scope and effectiveness of the control environment. Internal control is all about risk management. Risk is an inherent and unavoidable part of every financial decision a company makes. The goal of managing financial risk is to assess the degree of risk associated with each potential option, mathematically calculate the probability of it happening and determine whether the potential losses and probabilities associated with that risk are worth the potential returns. So on a broad level, risk is a cost for a company and no company can avoid all risk.

Internal controls are the methods that a business uses to safeguard its assets and reduce the likelihood of errors. While internal controls will not eliminate all risks of error and fraud, a strong set of internal controls will seek to minimize those risks. Strong internal controls can only give reasonable assurance that data and processes are reliable. For public companies, there is a requirement for these companies to report annually on internal controls within the company's corporate governance report.

The need for internal controls drives the creation of given structures for cross-balancing and accountability. For the most part, internal controls are put in place with policies and procedures. Remember that internal controls are not in themselves objectives, but frameworks for objectives to be met within. In order to keep accountability across an organization, there needs to be a separation of duties. In other words, the person who writes the checks should not be the person who signs the checks, or the person who sets the budget for office supplies should not be the same person who orders, etc. The four types of functional responsibilities that should be performed by different departments or different people within the same function are authority to execute transactions, recording transactions, custody of assets involved in the transactions and periodic reconciliations of the existing assets to recorded amounts. Another example is the Board of Directors having a balance of both internal and external board members, with their purpose being to execute decisions in the best interest of the shareholders. From the level of the Board of Directors throughout the entire organization, internal controls are designed to provide reasonable assurance regarding achievement of an organization's objectives involving effectiveness and efficiency of operations, reliability of financial reporting and compliance with applicable laws and regulations.

Most people are familiar with physical controls. These include lock and key, number pads and security cameras. These controls also extend to cover computer hardware and software such as changing passwords at regular intervals, good anti-virus software and firewalls. Personal use of assets can fall in to this category as well, such as having clear guidelines for business versus personal use of a company vehicle.

Two important types of controls are preventative controls and detective controls. They are just as they sound. Preventative controls are meant to stop problems before they arise while detective controls are meant to allow for the understanding of how something went wrong after the fact. Keep both of these in mind while looking at each area of internal control – you should have at least one preventative and one detective control for each area. This can give you better insight when you are trying to retrace some mystery in your data and assist you in creating stronger preventative controls in the future.

There are many different types of internal controls meant for a variety of protections, from data security to internet security, from disaster relief outcomes to input manipulation prevention. Below is a discussion of key internal controls for general consideration. Each company has a unique environment and needs to create what works for their organization.

Document retention is evidence of a transaction and allows for validation of the transaction. This also supports internal and external audits. Additionally, documents support reconciliations. Reconciliation will identify any differences in accounting and correct any errors found. Having a purchase ordering system in place can be viewed as a control by itself, but that is not enough. Purchase orders are, in essence, a legal document and tracking purchase orders gives a company accurate liability assessment as well as giving accounts receivable accurate knowledge of resources. Petty cash is one area that can cause a lot of problems, so be ready with numerous controls to put in place. This is an area where, because it is usually small amounts, people think there is more leeway, and that just leads to accounting nightmares. Controls are imperative for any company that has inventory of any kind. Being clear as to what the split-off points are, when inventory moves from one category to another on the balance sheets and what inventory is located where can all have significant impact on the bottom line of an organization. Invoicing also needs significant controls in place, especially when a company starts offering discount programs or credit. Payroll is an area that needs internal controls whether it is processed in-house or outsourced. Payroll is usually the largest expense for a small to medium sized company, so this is a vital area in which to implement strong controls. Human resources (HR) is a very sensitive area of any organization and the rules and regulations for HR just keep getting more complex. In general, HR personnel should be required by the company to take continuing education courses and have strong yet flexible controls to allow for a company to stay within all legal requirements while operating in a volatile legislative environment.

When it comes to internal controls, keep in mind that they are needed everywhere. In some cases, the same person may have been doing the same tasks for years and will not want to have internal controls, as they may take it to mean the company doesn't trust them. This is where training about the importance of internal controls for an organization becomes paramount and is usually the greatest source of "growing pains" for a company.

Ethical considerations for management accounting and financial professionals may be tested in conjunction with any topic area. The best way to prepare for this is to be intimately familiar with the latest IMA's Statement of Ethical Professional Practice and to be capable of evaluation and resolution of ethical issues. Be aware of current GAAP rules as well as any regulatory issues related to your industry when working with an organization. As for the CMA test, given that the IMA ethical statement can change with laws or regulations, this is all that this study guide will address for this portion on professional ethics.

Part 2: Financial Decision Making

Financial Statement Analysis

On the CMA test, you will need to demonstrate a mastery of working with and using financial statements. Make sure you are intimately comfortable with the following financial statements:

- Statement of Financial Position (Balance Sheet)
- Statement of Earnings (Income Statement) Statement of Cash Flows
- Statement of Changes in Shareholders' Equity.

All of the statements have unique relationships due to each statement's limitations, so make sure you are very comfortable with all of them.

The statement of financial position (also known as the balance sheet) illustrates the exact value of a company in the very moment the data is collected. Unlike other financial statements, the balance sheet does not compile data over time. Rather, it reports the value of all organizational assets, divided in to relevant categories, and then includes the value of the company's liabilities and owners' equity, each divided similarly into assets. The basic formula for the balance sheet is assets = liabilities + owners' equity. The total value of all assets equals the total value of all the liabilities plus all owners' equity. If the two sides of this equation don't balance, then someone did something wrong! Everything of value goes in to three primary categories, which are assets, liabilities or owners' equity. Assets include anything of value that currently belongs to the company or is currently owed to the company. Liabilities include the value of all the company's debt that must be repaid. Owners' equity includes all the value that the company holds for its stockholders. Remember that a company purchases all assets by using capital acquired through debt and selling equity, so the total assets must balance with the cumulative totals of the other portions of the balance sheet, liabilities and owners' equity. Each portion of the balance sheet begins with the items that are the most liquid at the top and as you work your way down each portion, the items included gradually become either illiquid or require repayment for longer periods of time. Current assets are those assets in which a company expects to turn in to cash within one year. The following current assets subcategories are listed from the most liquid to the least liquid. Cash and cash equivalents are the assets that a company can most easily turn in to cash (or already are cash). Marketable securities are the second-most liquid current asset a company has at its disposal. This includes banker's acceptances, certificates of deposit (CDs), treasury bills, and other types of financial products that have maturity dates but that an organization can withdraw from or sell very easily if necessary. The accounts receivable category includes the value of all money owed to an organization within the next year. The inventory category includes the value of all supplies that a company intends to use up during the process of making and selling something. Inventories include the raw materials used in production, work-in-progress products, end products ready for sale, and basic office supplies and goods consumed in production, such as stationery used in the office and oil carried on delivery trucks for regular maintenance. Income tax assets include two forms of income taxes: Income returns and deferred taxes. When a company pays for some expense in advance, the value of that prepayment becomes an asset called a prepaid account, for which the company will receive services in the future. Insurance is an example of a prepaid account. The other current assets category is common to see on the balance sheet but it means different things for different companies. Long-term assets are those assets that will take more than one year to turn in to cash or assets that are not intended to be sold, but can be sold if necessary.

There are three main categories of long-term assets: long-term investments; property, plant and equipment (PPE); and depreciation. Long-term investments typically include equities and debt investments held by an organization for financial gain, for gaining control over another company or in funds such as pensions. PPE includes nearly every major physical asset a company has that it will use for more than one year. The long-term assets in PPE do not last forever. With age and usage, every long-term physical asset is subject to depreciation, or a decrease in value. Intangible assets are things that add value to an organization but don't actually exist in physical form. Intangible assets primarily include the legal rights to some idea, image, or form and are considered a long-term asset on the balance sheet. The last asset category is the other assets. This is for any asset not yet listed somewhere else on the balance sheet, and can vary significantly from industry to industry.

Now, on to liabilities. Current liabilities are those that must be paid back, fully or in part, in less than one year. The following current liabilities subcategories are found on the balance sheet in order of those items that must be paid in the shortest period from when they were incurred to those that can be paid off in the longest period from when they were incurred. Accounts payable include any money that's owed for the purchase of goods or services that the company intends to pay within one year. Unearned income is when a company receives payment for a product or service but has yet to provide the goods or services it has paid for. Accrued compensation refers to the amount of money that employees have earned by working for the organization but haven't been paid yet. Until these people receive their paychecks, the amount the company owes them is a liability. Accrued expenses are similar and are applied to such expenses as rent, electricity, water, and any other expenses that a company incurs and pays on a regular basis. Deferred income tax is when a company chooses to report its income in a different period than when it actually earned the income. This can be useful for businesses that attempt to reduce tax expenses in any given year. Companies often pay long-term debt in small portions over the course of several years. This is called the current portion of long-term debt and labeled as such for the amount to be paid over the next year while being subtracted from the long-term liabilities. Other current liabilities include any liability that the company intends to pay over the next year that doesn't fall in to any of the other categories. Long-term liabilities are those that must be paid back in more than one year. Notes payable is the value of money that a company owes that it expects to pay back longer than in one year. This category includes all loans and debts; however, a company may choose to include any payments on bonds held for more than one year in a separate category called bonds payable. Capital lease obligations are when a company leases a piece of capital and the total amount owed on that lease adds to the value of this category of liabilities. Any other debts that a company must pay in a time period of more than one year and that doesn't fit elsewhere goes in to a category called other long-term liabilities. When looking at only the balance sheet, it shows only metrics related to value. But when you use it with information from the income statement and the statement of cash flows, you can determine how effectively a company is using its assets to generate income, as well as how well a company may use income to pay its debts.

The statement of earnings or the income statement is next. The income statement is a financial report that describes the revenues that a company makes and the costs it incurs in order to evaluate its profitability. There are two types of income statements: Single step and multiple step. Many companies prefer to use the single step type for minor reports that aren't quarterly or annual. The single step income statement doesn't separate costs and revenues by their source operations. It lists all income by breaking it down in to net sales and other, then lists all costs with a total of costs. Then it lists earnings before taxes and interest (EBIT), taxes, net income, and earnings per share (EPS). It is a shorter form of reporting but isn't as informative as the multiple step income statement. The rest of this income statement conversation will focus on the multiple step income statement. Income statements break down how much money it is making versus how much it is spending in to six main categories that separate them by source operations. The first portion of the income statement is gross profit, which seeks to calculate the profitability of a company's operations after direct costs with its ultimate goal being to determine the company's gross margin. This requires subtracting the costs of goods sold from the net sales. The next portion of the income statement is operating income. This takes in to account the rest of the company's costs of doing business (other than costs of goods sold) and has multiple components. The first is selling expense, which includes everything an organization spent on selling the products it bought or made, such as advertising, sales wages or commissions, shipping, etc. The next component is general and administrative costs (also called G&A costs) which cover all the expenses of running the company such as salaries for finance, marketing, human resources, and all other costs not directly tied to production. The last component is depreciation and amortization. The amount of depreciation listed on the income statement is the same as the amount incurred during a single period that gets added to the balance sheet. Be clear, however, that the depreciation and the amortization value on the income statement isn't the same value that appears on the balance sheet because the balance sheet is cumulative while the income statement only includes depreciation incurred in that year. To get the operating income, add up the all the costs listed in the three components and then subtract that number from the gross margin. Operating income represents the amount of money a company has left after it has paid for all its standard operations; you and your organization need to consider it when planning whether or not to expand, whether to use equity or debt to fund expansion, and how much money you can borrow and safely pay back using your primary operations.

The next portion of the income statement is Earnings Before Interest and Taxes (EBIT), which includes the following elements of other income, other expenses, and profit or loss for discontinued operations. The other income here is to account for income that falls outside of normal operations such as a company renting out the extra office space in their building. The other expenses here are to cover any outside expenses such as taxes but excluding income taxes (that goes in later.) The profit or loss for discontinued operations is exactly what it looks like. The amount of profit or loss experienced from stopping an operation or process goes here. You calculate EBIT by taking the gross margin and subtracting or adding the different sources of costs and revenues associated with non-primary business operations. The final portion of the income statement that lists costs and revenues is called net income and focuses only on taxes and interest. The focuses are interest income, interest expense and income tax expense. Interest income is where a company can earn interest when it has some types of bank accounts, when it owns bonds or other forms of debt on individuals or companies, or when it purchases money-market investments. A company can generate income expense when it borrows money from a bank or other organization or when it issues bonds. All the interest a company pays regardless of where the interest expense comes from goes in to this portion of the income statement. Companies must pay taxes on income like everyone else.

The amount of income taxes a company pays is based on their Earnings Before Taxes (EBT), which does not take interest into account. Many organizations list the percentage of income taxes in this section but it is not required.

The next portion of the income statement is where corporations have to include the amount of earnings each individual share of stock they have outstanding has generated, and this is called earnings per share (EPS). Calculate the basic EPS by dividing net earnings by the total number of common shares outstanding. This calculation tells how much money each share of stock earned during the period. Sometimes events occur that alter a company's income but there is no place to put it in the income statement, or an explanation is needed. This type of item goes in the supplemental notes portion of the income statement. Examples for needing to use this section include a switch from LIFO (last in, first out) inventory cost accounting to FIFO (first in, first out) inventory accounting, an unusual or infrequent event such as extra revenues from selling mineral rights on a building site, or any discontinued operations or unusual earnings from subsidiaries. The income statement is probably the most fundamental of all financial reports. The income statement is the final test of whether a company is succeeding or failing, and contributes to a number of metrics that measure how effectively a company's management manages its assets and how well the company yields returns on those assets.

The statement of cash flows is the financial record that tells all about the movement of cash into a company (inflows) and out of the company (outflows). Any transaction that appears in the balance sheet or income statement that influences cash must appear in the statement of cash flows. Not all transactions alter a company's cash flows but all transactions that do must be on this statement. Cash flows are divided into three separate categories based on the type of business activity that caused the transaction to take place, and will appear on the statement in this order:

- Operating activities
- Investing activities
- Financing activities

Each section, such as with operating activities, will list the transactions that increase cash followed by the transactions that decreased cash flow resulting from the primary functions of the organization. The end of each section will list the net cash flow as either positive or negative. Here are some of the most common changes in cash found in operating activities:

- Cash received from customers
- Cash paid to suppliers and employees
- Interest received
- Interest paid
- Income taxes paid

To calculate the net cash provided by operations, add up the positive values from the list of cash flows and subtract the negative values. This number usually appears at the end of the operational activities portion of the statement of cash flows. Any cash flow changes that result from investment assets belong in the investing activities cash flows portion of the statement of cash flows. This is whenever a company purchases or sells any form of investment and the cash flow results in either a gain or loss in cash from the total cash and equivalents (or breaks even). Some of the most common transactions that show up in this section are:

- Purchase of investments
- Proceeds from the sale of investments
- Purchase of PPE
- Proceeds from the sale of PPE

Just like for the operating activities, add up positive values and subtract negative values to get the net cash provided by investment activities. Financing refers to the process of acquiring capital to fund a startup, an expansion, basic operations or whatever else a company may need extra funds for. Most of the time changes in liabilities and owners' equity affect cash flow regardless of whether the company is acquiring or repaying the cash. The following types of financing activities show up in the financing activities portion of the statement of cash flows:

- Sale of securities
- Dividends payments
- Purchase of treasury shares
- Loans received
- Loans collected.

Add up the positive values and subtract the negative values to get the net cash provided by financing activities. Now add up all the net cash provided by the three types of company operations and you get the total amount of change to a company's cash and cash equivalents. Whether this value is positive or negative, it will appear on the balance sheet under the cash and cash equivalents label in the assets portion. The statement of cash flows is very important to lenders who are considering giving a company a loan. Data from the statement of cash flows can be used for the following:

- Measure a company's liquidity
- Measure the strength of a company's profitability
- Evaluate a company's operational asset management
- Evaluate a company's financial management regarding the company's costs of capital

Comparing data from the statement of cash flows for the same company over a period of years allows you to evaluate effective cash management and track sources of cash flows for the use of financial efficiency and asset utilization optimization.

Now that the basics, it is time to discuss analyzing statements. Financial analysis is an evaluation of a company's past financial performance and its prospects for the future which involves an analysis of the company's financial statements and cash flows. Financial statement analysis involves the calculation of various ratios. Cash flow analysis is an evaluation of the company's statement of cash flows in order to determine the impact that its sources and uses of cash have on the operations and financial condition of an organization. There are varying tools for measuring and evaluating the financial health of a business including horizontal, vertical and ratio analysis. You will use these tools to make two types of comparisons, industry and trend. Industry comparison takes the ratios of an organization and compares them with industry averages or norms to determine how the company is faring relative to its competitors. Trend analysis compares a company's present ratios with its past and expected future ratios to determine whether a company is improving or deteriorating financially over time.

Horizontal analysis is used to evaluate the trend in a company's accounts over the years. A $6 million profit year looks good after a $4 million profit year but not good after a $9 million profit year. Horizontal analysis is usually shown in comparative financial statements with five years in annual reports. With horizontal analysis, the focus is on the trends of various different accounts within an organization. It can be relatively easy to identify areas of wide divergence that require a closer look. It is important to show both the dollar difference and the percentage difference in this report as either number by itself could be misleading. A large change in dollar amount may result in only a small percentage change and not be cause for concern and vice versa. Comparative analysis of more than five years can become difficult to manage, so to avoid this difficulty, you can present the results by creating a base year and show comparisons to the base year chosen. Choose a year that is representative of the company's activities. Each account of the base year is assigned an index of 100. The index for each respective account in succeeding years is found by dividing the account's amount by the base year amount and multiplying by 100. This horizontal analysis is also known as trend analysis.

Vertical analysis is where a significant item on a financial statement is used as a base value and all other items are compared to it. In this analysis for the balance sheet, total assets assigned is 100% with each asset account being expressed as a percentage of total assets. Total liabilities and owners' equity is also given 100%. In the income statement, net sales is given the value of 100% and all other accounts are evaluated in comparison to net sales. These resulting figures create the common size statement. Vertical analysis is used to disclose the internal structure of an enterprise. This statement shows the existing relationship between each income statement account and revenue. It shows the mix of assets that produces the income and the mix of the sources of capital whether by current or long-term liabilities or by equity funding. The results are also used to evaluate the company's relative position in the industry.

Horizontal and vertical analysis compare one figure to another within a category. There is also an essential need to compare figures from different categories and this is accomplished through ratio analysis. Financial ratios are various and can be rather complex. These financial ratios can be classified in to five groups: liquidity ratios, activity ratios, leverage ratios, profitability ratios and market value ratios.

Liquidity ratios show an organization's ability to meet its current maturing short-term obligations. If liquidity is insufficient to cushion losses, serious financial problems can result. Insufficient liquidity is much like a person having a fever: It is a symptom of a fundamental problem. Liquidity ratios are static in nature as of year-end, so it is important for management to look at expected future cash flows as well. There are various liquidity measures such as net working capital, current ratio, quick test ratio and other liquidity ratios. Net working capital is equal to current assets less current liabilities. Net working capital is a safety cushion in the eyes of creditors. Net working capital and working capital are often used interchangeably. The current ratio is equal to current assets divided by current liabilities. This ratio is used to measure the ability of an organization to meet its current liabilities out of current assets. Be aware that this ratio is subject to seasonal fluctuations. A limitation of this ratio is that it may rise just prior to financial distress because of an organization's attempt to improve its cash position, for example selling fixed assets. This type of move on the part of the company can have a detrimental effect on productive capacity. Another limitation is that the current ratio will be excessively high when inventory is carried on the LIFO (last in, first out) basis. The quick ratio is also known as the acid test ratio. This is the most stringent test of liquidity. Divide the most liquid current assets (cash, marketable securities, and accounts receivable) by current liabilities. Inventory is not included because of the length of time it takes to convert to cash and prepaid expenses are not included because they are not convertible into cash. Two ratios remain inside of the other liquidity ratios listed above and they are the cash ratio and the cash burn rate. The cash ratio is also known as the doomsday ratio and you calculate it by dividing cash by current liabilities. This is the worst case scenario in that the business no longer exists. The cash burn rate is current assets divided by average daily operating expenses. This ratio is most relevant for start-up companies that often have little amounts of revenue.

Activity ratios show the movement of funds tied to actions in an organization by determining how quickly various accounts are converted into cash. In general, liquidity ratios do not give a clear picture of true liquidity because of differences in the kinds of current assets and liabilities a company holds. Thus, it is necessary to evaluate the activity or liquidity of specific current accounts. These ratios exist to measure the activity of receivables, inventory and total assets. Accounts receivable ratios consist of the accounts receivable turnover ratio and the average collection period. The first ratio (accounts receivable turnover ratio) gives the number of times accounts receivable is collected during the year. Divide net credit sales (or total sales) by the average accounts receivable. Average accounts receivable is usually found by adding the beginning and ending accounts receivable and dividing by two. The ratio is most accurate when the shortest period available is used. Typically, the higher the accounts receivable turnover, the better. This is because the company is collecting quickly from customers and can then invest these funds. An excessively high ratio may indicate that an organization's credit policy is too stringent with the company not tapping into the potential for profit through sales to customers in higher risk classes. In this case, a company needs to weigh the potential profit against the risk inherent in selling to more marginal customers. Inventory ratios are next in the activities ratios. The balance a company must strike between holding excess inventory and running too low on inventory can be troublesome. Inventory turnover is the cost of goods sold divided by average inventory. You should attempt to determine whether specific inventory categories are not selling well and if so, why not. A decline in the turnover rate would not be a reason for concern if the decline was due to the introduction of a new product line and advertising had not started yet, or if the effects of marketing weren't felt yet. The average age of inventory is 365 divided by inventory turnover. The length of this holding period may show a greater risk of products becoming obsolete.

The operating cycle is the time it takes to sell products and collect revenue on that sale, so a short operating cycle is desirable. The operating cycle equals the average collection period plus the average age of inventory. Cash conversion cycle (also known as cash cycle) is the measure of how well a company efficiently manages noncash working capital. Noncash working capital consists of current assets and liabilities other than cash. The cash conversion cycle is the number of days that pass before a company can collect the cash from the sale, measured from when a company actually pays for the inventory. The cash conversion cycle equals the operating cycle minus the accounts payable period. This ratio can give an indication as to whether money is being tied up in inventory and receivables. The total asset turnover ratio is useful in evaluating a company's ability to use its asset base efficiently to generate income. Total asset turnover equals net sales divided by average total assets. A low ratio here may be due to a multiple of factors so it is important to research further. For example, is investment in assets excessive when compared to the value of the output being produced? If this is the case, the organization may want to consolidate its present operation, possibly by selling some of its assets and investing the money from the sale for a higher return or using them to expand into a more profitable area.

There is an interrelationship of liquidity and activity to earnings. Liquidity risk is minimized by holding greater current assets than noncurrent assets but the rate of return will go down. On the other hand, high liquidity could mean that management has not searched for desirable capital investment opportunities. Keeping a balance between liquidity and return is important to the overall financial wellbeing of an organization. The impact of earnings activities on liquidity can be highlighted by comparing cash flows from operations to net income. If accounts receivable and inventory turnover are processed quickly, then the cash flow received can be invested for a return thus increasing net income (earnings.)

Leverage ratios shed light on what leverage resources are available and what possible risks the company is exposed to. Solvency is an organization's ability to meet maturing obligations as they come due without losing the ability to continue operations. This analysis focuses on the long-term financial and operating structure of the business. Solvency is dependent on profitability since in the end, an organization will not be able to meet its debts if it is not profitable. The debt ratio compares total debt (liabilities) to total assets. It shows the percentage of total funds obtained from creditors. The debt ratio equals total liabilities divided by total assets. The debt to equity ratio is an important measure of solvency because a high degree of debt in the capital structure might make it difficult for an organization to meet interest changes and principal payments at maturity, especially if that happens to coincide with adverse economic conditions. The debt to equity ratio is total liabilities divided by owners' equity. Remember that owners' equity is also known as stockholders' equity or shareholders' equity. This ratio can depend on many variables including the access to further financing, the rates of other companies in the industry, and the stability of earnings. The times interest earned (interest covered) ratio reflects the number of times before tax earnings cover interest expense. It is a safety margin indicator because it shows how much of a decline in earnings an organization can absorb. The times interest earned ratio equals EBIT divided by interest expense. A problem with this ratio is that it is based on EBIT (earnings before interest and taxes) which is not actually a measure of cash available to pay interest. The cash coverage ratio is a more accurate way to measure cash available to pay interest. Use earnings before interest, taxes and depreciation (EBITD) divided by interest to get the cash coverage ratio.

The efficiency and cash generating ability of a company can be measured by the cash coverage ratio and free cash flow. Free cash flow (FCF) is a measure of operating cash flows available for corporate purposes after providing fixed asset additions to maintain current productive capacity and dividends. This is calculated by taking the cash flow from operations minus cash used to purchase fixed assets minus cash dividends. All major credit rating agencies use a form of FCF in evaluating the credit worthiness of businesses. A company with sufficient FCF is able to retire debt, fund internal growth and have financial flexibility.

Profitability ratios show indication as to whether a company is in good financial health or not. Gross profit margin is the percentage of each dollar left over after the company has paid for its goods. Gross profit equals net sales minus the costs of goods sold. Gross profit margin equals gross profit divided by net sales. The profit margin is the ratio of net income divided by net sales. This indicates the profitability generated from revenue so it is an important measure of operating performance but it can also provide clues to an organization's pricing, production efficiency and cost structure. Return on investment (ROI) is a key measure of performance but it has limitations. ROI shows the percentage to which earnings are achieved on the investment made however that actual value of earnings tends to be distorted. There are two ratios that evaluate ROI with one being the return on total assets (ROA) and the other being the return on owners' equity (ROE). ROA is a measure of overall earning power (profitability) that shows the amount earned on each dollar of assets invested. ROA equals net income divided by average total assets. The Du Pont formula shows the relationship between the profit margin and ROA. The relationship is ROA equals profit margin multiplied by total asset turn over. Which means that net income divided by average total assets equals net income divided by net sales multiplied by net sales divided by average total assets. This formula shows that the ROA can be increased by either the profit margin or the asset turn over. ROE (also known as return on common equity) is a measure of how much income was earned on each dollar invested by stockholders. ROE equals net income divided by average stockholders' equity. ROA and ROE are closely related through the equity multiplier (the use of leverage or debt ratio). In using the equity multiplier, ROE equals ROA multiplied by total assets divided by common equity or ROE equals ROA divided by 1 minus debt ratio. The appropriate use of leverage when evaluating profitability is vital.

When looking at profitability, remember that not all earnings are created equal. If a source of earnings is volatile, uncertain or temporary then the quality of the earnings goes down. There are two primary things that can undermine the quality of earnings listed on the financial statements, choices of different accounting methods and the sources of revenue and costs. A company may seem to be generating earnings; however, that doesn't mean that the corporation is successful or that it isn't at risk of going out of business in the near future.

Market value ratios shows how a company is performing compared to the known market place by relating the company's stock price to its earnings (or book value) per share and includes dividend related ratios. Earnings per share expresses the amount of earnings for each common share held. When preferred stock is included in the capital structure, net income needs to be reduced by the preferred dividends. If preferred stock does not exist, earnings per share equals net income divided by common shares outstanding. This can be used for evaluating operating performance and to estimate dividends expected. The next ratio is used to evaluate a company's relationship with its stockholders. Price per earnings (P/E) is equal to the market price per share of stock divided by the earnings per share. A high P/E multiple indicates that the investing public holds the organization in a favorable light.

Book value per share is net assets available to common shareholders divided by shares outstanding, where net assets is stockholders' equity minus preferred stock. Another indication of how investors view the firm is to compare the book value per share with the market price per share. A major goal for any organization is to optimize wealth maximization. This is reached by maximizing the difference between the market value of the company's stock and the amount of equity capital supplied by shareholders and is called market value added (MVA). There are two dividend ratios and they are dividend yield and dividend payout. Dividend yield equals dividends per share divided by market price per share. Dividend payout equals dividends per share divided by earnings per share.

If an organization is determining the value of an asset, be clear about the differences between book value and market value. Book value is the undepreciated portion of the original cost of a fixed asset and is also known as the carrying value. Market value is what someone is willing to pay for something in the current market place. These can be two very different numbers and are affected by multiple factors. Both values may not even be needed in some situations as in the example of outdated machinery that cannot be sold or have any monies recovered from it.

In general, ratios can give an organization a different perspective on what is going on both within and outside the company but ratios have their limitations as well. Ratios are based on averages and if you are not doing specific analysis as well you could be missing internal issues that could be costing your organization. Many large organizations participate in multiple types of business so it can be difficult to identify the industry group of the organization, which would make comparing their ratios to other corporations possibly useless. Operating and accounting practices also differ from company to company which can affect the ratios and make comparisons useless. Published industry ratios are only approximations. Financial statements are based on historical data and do not take inflation into account. Management may hedge or exaggerate their financial figures, once again distorting ratios. Ratios do not describe the quality of its components, so the current ratio may be high but the inventory may consist of obsolete goods, for instance. Ratios are static and do not consider future trends. This list is not all the limitations of ratios, but you see that they are not "set in stone."

Be prepared to demonstrate and explain all components and purposes for all financial statements on the CMA test. This includes having a strong understanding of typical timeframes and even some basic formatting expectations. Financial statement analysis is the foundation for the next testing sections.

Corporate finance is the study of relationships between groups of people that quantifies the otherwise immeasurable. Not the easiest definition to grasp; however, it means the world to your organization! Looking at the world around your organization sheds light on the risks involved everywhere, including those outside of your company's control.

Systematic risk (market risk,) for example, is the risk of the national (or these days, global) economy entering a recession. Unsystematic risk (company or corporate risk) is the risk of losses or costs associated with business operations. There are many risks that corporate finance looks for. Interest rate/inflation risk is the risk that interest rates or inflation will outpace your returns. Credit risk is the risk that a borrower won't repay a loan. Off-balance sheet risk is the risk that something not included on the balance sheet is influencing corporate value such as unrealized gains or losses from derivative investing. Foreign exchange risk is the risk of losing value through fluctuations in foreign exchange rates. Liquidity risk is the risk of not having enough money on hand when bills become due.

The way to mitigate any risk is to counterbalance the risk through portfolio diversification. When several different investments are lumped in to one portfolio, every single investment has an influence on the portfolio. This still requires some sort of measurement of risk, which is complicated and a matter of significant disagreement within the financial community.

When managing a portfolio, you need to look at the individual investments, and this usually begins with a calculation called the capital asset pricing model (CAPM). The goal is to assess whether an investment is worth purchasing by determining the rate of returns and the risk compared to the risk-free rate of return. In the CAPM formula, you will find a beta symbol; however, it is not a measurement of risk, but of volatility. That means that a particular investment can fluctuate far above normal market returns and still be considered low risk. It can also mean that another investment can be consistently only 0.01 percent under market returns and still be considered high risk.

Arbitrage pricing theory (APT) is significantly more flexible and effective than CAPM. APT looks for differentials in the market price of a single investment and what the market price of the same investment actually should be. This is unlike CAPM, which is concerned with returns on a market portfolio.

Now, let's look at stock assets. Common stock in a corporation allows you to be a partial owner of the company so you get voting rights in major decisions. You also have a right to dividend payments, which are profit returns to company owners when issued. If the company whose shares you own goes through liquidation, which is selling assets after going out of business, common shareholders get whatever is left after the lenders and the preferred stockholders are paid what they are owed. If you hold preferred stock in a company, you get your dividend payouts in full before common shareholders get paid and this includes liquidation. However, preferred stockholders do not have voting rights so they have no control over the actions a company takes. Once a company issues common stock, the company has the opportunity to repurchase those shares on the secondary market. When this happens, the shares are called treasury shares. Companies prefer to do this because they can generate income and it allows them to more effectively manage their stock price.

Derivatives are legal contracts that set the terms of a transaction as the current marketplace varies against the contract terms. These were originally intended to bringing price stability to products that can be volatile in price over short periods. Prices can change quite a lot over time, which adds a degree of uncertainty and risk for those who either produce or purchase large quantities of goods. There are four general types of derivatives:

- *Options* – these are contracts that give the buyer the right to buy or sell a fixed number of goods at a predetermined price, but they do not require them to do so. There are two main types of options. Put options, when purchased, give the holder the right to sell a predetermined unit quantity of some asset at a predetermined price, called the strike price, before some predetermined future date, called the expiration date. Call options are similar to put options except that they give the buyer the right to purchase. When an option holder chooses to use the option to buy or sell that is called exercising the option.

- *Forward* –an agreement between parties to perform a sale of a specific type of good in a predetermined quantity at a predetermined price at a predetermined date in the future. Forward contracts are legal obligations to perform the transaction on or before the specified date and are very customizable. Forwards are not bought and sold in the same way as the other derivatives because they are usually created between two or more parties that intend to fulfill on the transaction. A forward contract is made to reduce the amount of price uncertainty and volatility involved with buying and selling goods.

- *Future* – futures are similar to forwards except that all the contracts of like goods are standardized by type, quality, quantity, delivery date and even currency by location of the trade. This makes futures very liquid when sold in very high volume and very high frequency on markets, much like stocks. It is very common to use futures as a form of risk management. The initial contract sale by the producers is sold on the primary market then traded on the secondary market by investors and will eventually be sold to the people who really do want the goods.

- Swaps are the most confusing of the derivative methods. Swaps involve two agreements instead of just one. They occur when corporations agree to exchange something of value with the expectation of exchanging back at a future date. Organizations can use swaps on a variety of different things of value and usually it is currency or specific types of cash flows. This allows organizations to quickly shift the performance of their assets without losing ownership rights of those assets.

A quick side note on working capital. Working capital is a metric that tells a company what their net value is in the short term. In other words, if you paid off your credit cards, what would be left in your bank account? Subtract current liabilities from current assets to find your organization's working capital. This is important for a company to be aware of, because how can a company invest in anything if they don't have any available funds to do so?

There are numerous marketable securities that organizations can invest in. Take a look at some specific federal government bonds. Treasury bonds (T-bonds) are types of government debt that mature in 1 to 30 years. Maturing a bond means a bond that has reached the date that the borrower must repay the full amount of the bond plus interest. Treasury notes (T-notes) are short term notes that last from two to ten years and are worth $100 to $5 million, in $100 increments. Treasury bills (T-bills) have the shortest maturity rate at less than one year. T-bills tend to have very low annual returns and have a face value starting at $100. Because the term is so short, T-bills are considered risk-free.

Of all the securities mentioned, knowing where to look for them and how the institutions work is important. Securities firms provide transaction services related to financial investments that are unique from traditional banking/depository institutions. Many commercial banks have investment departments or actually partner with securities firms to provide investment services and products. Investment banks work exclusively with corporations and other businesses as clients. They offer a wide range of services all related to raising or transferring capital such as underwriting services, broker-dealer services for both primary and secondary markets, merger and acquisition services, corporate reorganization and bankruptcy procedures and other such related services.

One way large corporations can raise money is through private placements or public offerings. Private placements are when a company informs people in a known circle of people that it is raising funds. Private placements can happen any number of ways but cannot be advertised. Public offerings are typically called an Initial Public Offering (IPO). This is when a company chooses to create more stock and sell it to outside investors. It is called an IPO because it is the first time the stocks are being sold and the only time the company will actually make money on the sale of the shares. Once the stocks are purchased from the company, the stocks can be sold an infinite number of times on the stock exchanges which technically is the secondary market. A company can have multiple IPOs if they go through all the Securities and Exchange Commission (SEC) steps each time. The age of the company does not necessarily matter.

When working with decision analysis and risk management, an important issue to keep in mind is the opportunity costs of the company's decisions. Opportunity costs are the benefits lost when a company choses one alternative over another, and arise when the choice of one course of action eliminates the possibility of another course of action.

A critical decision all companies must make is setting the price for their products or services. This is primarily done with marginal costs and marginal revenues. Marginal cost is the change in total cost caused by one unit change in output. Marginal revenue is the change in total revenue caused by one unit change in output. Plotting marginal costs and marginal revenues on a graph at various activity levels gives a visual representation of where the ideal price would be. If all the information used to compute the graph were certain, then picking the optimal price would be easy. However most data used for these computations are based on assumptions of projected amounts for product costs, unit sales and revenues.

Make-or-buy decisions are another area for critical analysis. These decisions are about whether to make a part internally or buy it from an external supplier. This include outsourcing whole operating activities such as warehousing. In an attempt to improve operating income and compete on the global market, accurate and detailed analysis of make-or-buy decisions are imperative to an organization reaching their earnings and sales objectives both in short term and long term perspectives. These decisions have a direct effect on price setting as well.

Target costing is a pricing method that identifies the price at which a product will be competitive in the marketplace, defines the desired profit to be made on the product and computes the target cost for the product by subtracting the target price from the competitive market price. The desired profit is also known as the target price because it is the production cost plus desired profit thus creating the target price.

To belabor the point, always be aware of inherent risks, and look for other potential risks that may not seem obvious upon first review. Useyour balanced score card as a platform to manage risk along with an enterprise risk management system (ERM). ERMs identify events that may affect a business and help manage them so that they are deemed ethical and provide reasonable assurance that the business will achieve its objectives. The linking of measures, goals and targets from multiple different departments and perspectives is the key.

"Risk management is the art of using lessons from the past in order to mitigate misfortune and exploit future opportunities – in other words, the art of avoiding stupid mistakes of yesterday while recognizing that nature can always create new ways for things to go wrong." – K.A.C. Manderville

Risk management must be addressed from all levels of an organization even when a risk management department exists. Risk management is an art of managing people, institutions and process while it is the science of measuring and quantifying risk. There is some argument that risk measurement is not the same as risk management. The focus of passive measurement and monitoring of risk in comparison to the focus of active management of risk that drives company decisions. Risk measurement is necessary for risk management. Risk measurement is the specialized task of quantifying and communicating risk and this should be accomplished at all levels of an organization. A uniform process for risk measurement across a firm provides immense benefits that are not available when companywide and desk-level risk are treated on a different basis. Risk reporting needs to be tailored appropriately to the needs of each department. However, the measurement process needs uniformity. Having a dedicated risk management department can mislead managers in to thinking that somehow their responsibility to manage risk is lessened. In other words, there should no more be a risk department than there should be a profits department. Everyone in the organization needs to be aware of the importance of risk measurement and management.

Recent technological advances allow for greater and more sophisticated analytical tools for managerial quantitative analysis. These new advances can be embraced and exploited to both manage risk and more effectively make the most of opportunities. The value of these tools, however, should not be overemphasized. One problem with current advancements is that it can lead to far too much focus on measurement and neglect *managing* the risk. Managing risk requires experience and intuition in addition to quantitative measures. The advanced technology tools of today are invaluable aids that help to formalize and standardize a process that would otherwise operate on rules of thumb and hunches, but they are no substitute for informed judgment. Risk management is as much about apprenticeship and learning by doing as it is about book learning. This can apply to all levels of management where an experienced manager is simply more valuable than someone fresh out of college because of the hands-on practice needed to handle basic management functions quickly and efficiently.

The ultimate goal of risk management is to build a robust yet flexible organization and set of processes. The truth is that advanced quantitative tools often fail to capture those unanticipated events that pose the most risk to an organization. Managing risk for disasters, tail events or crises requires combining all types of risk – market risk, credit risk, liquidity risk and operational risk among others. Typically, disasters or crises result from the confluence of multiple events and causes. Examples include the collapse of Barings Bank in 1995 and the same firm's collapse in 1890. Risk management is about bringing all forms of risk together while building a culture and organization that can respond to and withstand these unanticipated events. It must also incorporate the ability to capitalize on new opportunities.

Managing risk is hard, just like managing any aspect of a business. However, it can be made easier by having well-planned strategies. A good risk management strategy is simple to state yet often difficult to carry out. Learn about the risks in general and learn about the business and the people. Learn about specific exposures and risks while learning about the details of the portfolio. Manage people, process and organization while focusing on group dynamics and the human factor. Implement damage control strategies to minimize the impact when and if disaster or crises strike.

The true essence of risk management is to provide a realistic view of what could happen in the future, mainly in what could happen to the organization's profit and loss. This is not predicting the specifics of the future as in "the firm will earn $300,000" or "it will lose $50,000" but instead providing informed judgments about the range or distribution of possible outcomes. Predicting the future is not possible, but learning about the range of future possibilities is not only possible, it is something we do every day. Take the weather, for example. We cannot predict the exact temperature for the day but given a location and time of year, we can say with significant confidence a range the temperature is likely to be. Just like we cannot predict next year's profits and losses, we can say how likely it might be to lose $100,000 versus $10,000,000.

In providing informed statistical distributions, there are two features to focus on: Location on one hand, and scale or dispersion on the other hand. Location quantifies the central tendency or some sort of typical value. Scale or dispersion quantifies the spread of possible values around the central value. When it comes to risk, the most important characteristic is the dispersion or spread of the dispersion, mainly because the dispersion of profits and losses is large relative to the typical value. These summary measures are incredibly useful but we have to remember that they are arbitrary to some degree and vary in usefulness in certain situations, depending on circumstances. Risk itself is not a precise concept and depends on investor or company preferences with different investors or companies viewing the same investment differently. Given that what we are trying to measure (risk) is rather vague, the summary measures themselves are necessarily arbitrary. Using these measures requires common sense, experience and judgment.

Volatility is the most common measure of location and scale, which is defined as the average of squared deviations from the mean. Volatility is also known as the standard deviation. The standard deviation is one dispersion measure relevant for risk management that is well known and widely used. For every possible profit, we calculate the distance from the mean, square that distance, and take the average of the squares. The volatility is effectively an average of deviations from the mean. The greater the dispersion around the mean, the larger the volatility will be.

Value at Risk, or VaR, is another common summary measure. VaR is a quantile – that is, the point on the horizontal axis that some fixed fraction of the dispersion is below that point. A quantile is characterized by two numbers:

1.) A probability level Z defined by the user and
2.) A resulting level of profit or loss Y.

The definition of VaR_Z is as follows: the P&L level Y such that there is a probability Z that the P&L will be worse than Y and a probability of $1 - Z$ that it will be better than Y.

The P&L is measured over some fixed measure of. In the example of $VaR_{5\%}$ this is the point on the horizontal axis chosen so that the probability, the area under the curve Y, is 5%. The VaR idea is simple. The level of loss is specified in such a way that a worse loss happens with a predefined probability. VaR is often referred to as "worst-case loss" or "statistically worst-case loss." This is a misleading term and misleading idea. By definition, there is a probability that losses will be worse than VaR. No matter what value you might choose as the "statistically worse-case loss" sometime, somewhere it will be worse. So instead think of VaR not as a "worse-case" but rather a regularly occurring event with which a company needs to be comfortable. VaR is a measure of the tail of the distribution. There is large variability and uncertainty in tail events, so VaR must be used with special caution, in particular when the probability of Z is low. Tail events are by their nature rare, and thus hard to measure. The farther out one goes in the tail, the rarer tail events become.

All estimates of volatility and VaR are based on how the portfolio would have behaved under certain historical conditions. This kind of history-based number may not predict the future behavior of the portfolio. Understanding how the portfolio would have behaved under past circumstances provides valuable information and insight, because understanding the past is the first step toward understanding what might happen in the future. Volatility and VaR both have their strengths and weaknesses. Volatility uses all the observations, which is a good thing. It is very useful when the distribution is symmetrical, the focus is mainly on the central part of the distribution and the extremes in the tails are either well behaved or not of primary importance. Volatility will be less useful for a nonsymmetrical distribution or if the focus is specifically on the tails of the distribution. VaR focuses specifically on the tails of the distribution which is also a good thing. VaR is popular as a risk measure because it provides a succinct summary of large losses (tail events) in a manner that is simple to understand and explain. The units are P&L in terms of dollars and returns which are exactly what units that a trader, manager, or investor would use. This simplicity is also VaR's greatest weakness. Risk can never be fully summarized by a single number. There is strong temptation with organizations to take such a number as the final word when, in reality, it should be only a start towards a deeper understanding of the variability and uncertainty inherent in future outcomes. Volatility or VaR will tell something about the distribution but as with any summary measure, it may hide as well as reveal information.

Extreme value theory (EVT) is another alternative for handling tail or extreme events, which is the study of the asymptotics of tail events. Asymptotics in general is the study of probability as the number of events increases. It is the core of frequency-type probability and has provided the foundation of much of modern probability and statistics. The law of large numbers and the central limit theorem are known to most everyone and are the premier examples of the application of asymptotic methods. They provide the tools necessary to study the sum and average of a sequence of random variables as the number of observations get large. For the most part, they say that the average will ultimately settle down and that it will behave the same no matter what the distribution of the variables (within some limits). The great thing about the law of large numbers and central limit theorem is that they hold true no matter what the distribution of the underlying random numbers are, as long as the random variables do not have too much chance of being too large – for example if they have finite mean and variance. So the central limit theorem studies the average of a sequence. In contrast, EVT is an asymptotic theory that examines the maximum (or related characteristics) of a sequence – that is, the tails of a distribution. With this, EVT provides tools and techniques well suited for analyzing VaR and tail events. Just as the average settles down when we increase the number of observations, so the maximum settles down (when appropriately normalized). The central limit theorem says that the average will be normally distributed. EVT says that the maximum (normalized) will be distributed according to a different distribution, known as the generalized extreme value (GEV) distribution.

The normal distribution is a bell-shaped symmetrical distribution and is commonly used to represent P&L distributions. It is characterized by two parameters, the mean and the standard deviation. The mean gives the location – where the distribution is centered. The standard deviation gives the spread or dispersion. For most risk measurement purposes, companies are primarily concerned with the dispersion as measured by the standard deviation (or volatility) and will ignore the mean or assume it is zero.

Managing risk requires actually making decisions as to whether or not to alter the profile of risk. These decisions require knowing not just the level of risk (the dispersion of the P&L distribution) but also sources of risk in the portfolio as well as how changes in positions are likely to alter the portfolio risk. Decision analysis and risk management go hand in hand. You cannot perform accurate decision analysis without taking risk in to account and you cannot manage risk appropriately if you do not have a reason for making a risk decision.

Investment decisions on a corporate level mainly have to deal with capital investments. Capital investment analysis, also known as capital budgeting, is the process of making decisions about capital investments such as buildings and equipment. These decisions can be about purchasing new buildings and equipment (facilities), replacing old buildings or equipment (facilities) and even resource commitments in the form of new product development, market research, refunding of long-term debt, etc. The process for investment decisions (capital budgeting) comprises of establishing the need for the capital investment, analyzing courses of action to meet the need, preparing reports, choosing the best options and allocating funds among competing needs. This whole process involves every part of the organization and affects both short term and long term planning. Most companies have a long-term projection of operations of five to ten years out and large capital investments should be included in these projections, such as additions or changes in product line, replacement of equipment and acquisition of other companies. Although capital investment decisions affect an organization for years to come, it is also discussed for years beforehand. Estimates of future revenues and expenditures are made when the long-term plan is first developed. The capital investment analysis is done in the same period as when the expenditure will be made. Understanding these timeframe differences is important in leading an organization through the capital budgeting process. Capital rationing is used to deal with selecting the mix of acceptable projects that provide the highest overall net present value (NPV).

There are two main discounted cash flow (DCF) methods, net present value (NVP) and internal rate of return (IRR). NVP is the excess of the present value (PV) of cash inflows generated by the project over the amount of initial investment (I). The present value of future cash flows is computed using the cost of capital (or minimum required rate of return). If the NVP is positive, accept the project otherwise reject it. The NVP method recognizes the time value of money and is easy to compute whether the cash flows form an annuity or vary from period to period. The shortcomings of NVP is that it requires detailed long-term forecasts of incremental cash flow data. IRR is defined as the rate of interest that equates I with PV of future cash flows. In other words, at IRR, I = PV or NVP = 0. Accept the project if the IRR exceeds the cost of capital, otherwise reject. The advantage of IRR is that it does consider the time value of money, which makes it more exact and realistic than ARR (see below). The shortcomings of IRR is that it is difficult to compute, especially when the cash flows are not even and it fails to recognize the varying size of investment in competing projects and their respective dollar profitability. The profitability index is the ratio of the total PV of future cash flows to the initial investment. The index is used as a means of ranking projects in descending order of attractiveness. If the profitability index is greater than 1, accept the project. DCF methods can be used to analyze acquisitions, stocks and divestitures.

Another method for evaluating capital investment is through a payback period. A payback period measures the length of time required to recover the amount of initial investment. The payback period is determined by dividing the amount of initial investment by the cash flow through increased revenues or cost savings. The payback period is determined by trial and error if the cash flows are not even. When two or more projects are being considered, choose the one with the shortest payback period because the shorter the payback period, the less risky the project and the greater liquidity. As with any method, using the payback period has its advantages and disadvantages. The advantages are it is simple to compute and easy to understand while handling investment risk effectively. The shortcomings are it does not recognize the time value of money and it ignores the impact of cash flows after the payback period. It is the cash flows after the payback period that determine the profitability of an investment.

Accounting rate of return (ARR) measures profitability from the conventional accounting point of view by relating the required investment (or the average investment) to the future annual net income. Using this method, you should choose the project with the highest rate of return. The advantage of ARR is that it is easily understood, simple to compute and recognizes the profitability factor. The shortcomings are that it fails to recognize the time value of money and it uses accounting data instead of cash flow data.

Investment decisions have an immense impact on a company's long-term operational capabilities. Everything from cash flow management to how to pay back debt can be influenced by appropriate investment decisions, so keep this in mind and be clear about how intimately and profoundly investment decisions (capital budgeting) can affect your organization.

When it comes to professional ethics in the Financial Decision Making section of the CMA test, remember that ethics may be tested in conjunction with any other material. Make sure you are proficient with the purpose and practices of the US Foreign Corrupt Policies Act. Be clear of any relevant changes to the IMA's Statement on Management Accounting "Values and Ethics: From inception to practice." Make certain that you can speak to the importance of a company having a Code of Ethics, and how these ethical values bring benefit to the company. You will need to demonstrate an understanding of the relationship between ethics and internal controls. The comprehensive framework of ethical corporate behavior is a prerequisite for an effective system of internal control.

Part 3: After the Test

Once you have passed your CMA exam you have a few more steps to take.

1. Download the CMA Experience Requirement Verification Form to complete it and turn it in to IMA.
2. By now, if you have not already, you must provide your educational qualification proof.
3. Once your education and experience are verified, you will be issued your CMA certificate number and may begin using the CMA designation.
4. The actual certificate will come within a two to three week window in the mail.
5. With the certificate you will also receive a booklet called "Rights and Responsibilities" as a new certificate holder.
6. Begin planning your Continuing Professional Education (CPE) to fulfil your annual requirements.

Continuing Professional Education (CPE)

Once you have completed the above steps 1-5, you must start to fulfill the annual requirement of 30 hours of CPE with 2 hours being on Ethics. CPE credits are verified on a random basis so keep any CPE certificates and any other supporting documentation for at least two years. It is always a good idea to check the current requirements and rules for your CPE credits so as not to accidentally lose your hard earned designation. There are a variety of programs and events throughout the year held in varying locations and by multiple different companies so there are ample opportunities to complete your CPE requirements each year.

CMA Champions

There is a close social community for those who would like to be more active within the CMA community called CMA Champtions. The community offers members the opportunity to connect and network with other skilled professionals in getting full value from the CMA designation. The CMA designation is an asset in building your personal professional brand so use the community to make sure you get the most value possible!

Additional Resources

Suggested Reading List for the CMA Curriculum as given by the IMA website (www.imanet.org):

PART 1: Financial Planning, Performance and Control

Planning, Budgeting and Forecasting

Blocher, Edward, J., Stout, David E., Juras, Paul E., and Cokins, Gary, *Cost Management: A Strategic Emphasis*, 6th edition, McGraw Hill, New York, NY, 2013.

Horngren, Charles T., Datar, Srikant, Rajan, Madhav, *Cost Accounting: A Managerial Emphasis*, 14th edition, Prentice-Hall, Upper Saddle River, NJ, 2012.

Anderson, David, R., Sweeney, Dennis J., Williams, Thomas A., Camm, Jeff, and Martin, R. Kipp, *Quantitative Methods for Business*, 11th Edition, Mason, Ohio: South Western, 2010.

Performance Management

Blocher, Edward, J., Stout, David E., Juras, Paul E., and Cokins, Gary, *Cost Management: A Strategic Emphasis*, 6th edition, McGraw Hill, New York, NY, 2013.

Horngren, Charles T., Datar, Srikant, Rajan, Madhav, *Cost Accounting: A Managerial Emphasis*, 14th edition, Prentice-Hall, Upper Saddle River, NJ, 2012.

Cost Management

Blocher, Edward, J., Stout, David E., Juras, Paul E., and Cokins, Gary, *Cost Management: A Strategic Emphasis*, 6th edition, McGraw Hill, New York, NY, 2013.

Horngren, Charles T., Datar, Srikant, Rajan, Madhav, *Cost Accounting: A Managerial Emphasis*, 14th edition, Prentice-Hall, Upper Saddle River, NJ, 2012.

Internal Controls

Simkin, Mark G., Rose, Jacob M., Norman, Carolyn S., *Core Concepts of Accounting Information Systems*, 12th edition, John Wiley & Sons, Hoboken, NJ, 2012.

Bodnar, George, H., and Hopwood, William S., *Accounting Information Systems*, 10th edition, Prentice-Hall, Upper Saddle River, NJ, 2010.

Sawyer, Lawrence B., Dittenhofer, Mortimer A., and Graham, Anne, eds., 2003. Sawyer's Internal Auditing: *The Practice of Modern Internal Auditing*, 5th edition, IIA, Altamonte Springs, FL, 2003.

Professional Ethics

IMA, 2005, IMA Statement of Ethical Professional Practice, http://www.imanet.org/ethicscenter.

Part 2: Financial Decision Making

Financial Statement Analysis

Mackenzie, Bruce, Coetsee, Danie, Njikizana, Tapiwa, Chamboko, Raymond, Colyvas, Blaise, and Hanekom, Brandon, *2012 Interpretation and Application of International Financial Reporting Standards*, John Wiley & Sons, Hoboken, NJ, 2012.

Gibson, Charles H., *Financial Reporting & Analysis*, 13th edition, South-Western Cengage Learning, Mason, OH, 2013.

Subramanyam, K.R., and Wild, John L., *Financial Statement Analysis*, 10th edition, McGraw Hill, New York, NY, 2009.

Corporate Finance

Brealey, Richard, A., Myers, Stewart C., and Allen, Franklin, *Principles of Corporate Finance*, 10th edition, McGraw Hill, New York, NY, 2011.

Van Horn, James, C., and Wachowicz, John M. Jr., *Fundamentals of Financial Management*, 13th edition, FT / Prentice Hall, Harlow, England, 2009.

Decision Analysis and Risk Management

Blocher, Edward, J., Stout, David E., Juras, Paul E., and Cokins, Gary, *Cost Management: A Strategic Emphasis*, 6th edition, McGraw Hill, New York, NY, 2013.

Horngren, Charles T., Datar, Srikant, Rajan, Madhav, *Cost Accounting: A Managerial Emphasis*, 14th edition, Prentice-Hall, Upper Saddle River, NJ, 2012.

COSO, The Committee of Sponsoring Organizations of the Treadway Commission, 2004. Enterprise Risk Management – Integrated Framework.

Moeller, Robert R., COSO *Enterprise Risk Management*, 2nd edition, John Wiley & Sons, Inc., Hoboken, NJ, 2011.

IMA, 2006, Enterprise Risk Management: Frameworks, Elements, and Integration, http://www.imanet.org/SMA (members only)

IMA, 2007, Enterprise Risk Management: Tools and Techniques for Effective Implementation, http://www.imanet.org/SMA (members only)

Investment Decisions

Brealey, Richard, A., Myers, Stewart C., and Allen, Franklin, *Principles of Corporate Finance*, 10th edition, McGraw Hill, New York, NY, 2011.

Van Horn, James, C., and Wachowicz, John M. Jr., *Fundamentals of Financial Management*, 13th edition, FT / Prentice Hall, Harlow, England, 2009.

Professional Ethics

IMA, 2008, Values and Ethics: From Inception to Practice http://www.imanet.org/SMA (members only)

United States Department of Justice, A Resource Guide to the U.S. Foreign Corrupt Practices Act, http://www.justice.gov/criminal/fraud/fcpa/guide.pdf

TOPIC/RESOURCE OUTLINE

Part 1: Financial Planning, Performance and Control

A. Planning, Budgeting and Forecasting (30%)

1. Budgeting concepts: Blocher, Chapter 10; Horngren, Chapter 6

2. Forecasting techniques: Anderson, Chapter 6

3. Budgeting methodologies: Blocher, Chapters 10; Horngren, Chapters 6-8

4. Annual profit plan and supporting schedules: Blocher, Chapter 9, 10; Horngren, Chapters 6-8

5. Top-level planning and analysis: Blocher, Chapter 11, Horngren, Chapter 6

B. Performance Management (25%)

1. Cost and variance measures: Blocher, Chapters 14, 16; Horngren, Chapters 7, 8, 19, 22, 23

2. Responsibility centers and reporting segments: Blocher, Chapters 18, 19; Horngren, Chapters 6, 7, 8, 14, 15, 22, 23

3. Performance measures: Blocher, Chapters 5; Horngren, Chapters 13, 23

C. Cost Management (25%)

1. Measurement concepts: Blocher, Chapters 14, 15, 16; Horngren, Chapters 2, 4, 9, 10, 16

2. Costing systems: Blocher, Chapters 3, 4, 5, 6; Horngren, Chapters 4, 5, 17, 20

3. Overhead costs: Blocher, Chapter 7; Horngren, Chapters 4, 5, 8, 14, 15

4. Operational Efficiency: Blocher, Chapters 13; Horngren, Chapters 3, 9

5. Business process performance: Blocher, Chapters 2; Horngren, Chapters 22, 23

D. Internal Controls (15%)

1. Risk assessment, controls, and risk: Sawyer, Chapters 2, 3; management: Simkin, Chapter 9; Bodnar, Chapters 5, 6

2. Internal auditing: Sawyer, Chapter 1

3. Systems controls and security measures: Sawyer, Chapters 13-15; Simkin, Chapters 6, 10, 11; Bodnar, Chapters 5, 6, 13

E. Professional Ethics (5%)

1. Ethical considerations for the professional IMA's "Statement of Ethical Professional Practice"

Part 2- Financial Decision Making

A. Financial Statement Analysis (25%)

1. Basic financial statement analysis: Gibson, Chapters 2-5; Subramanyam, Chapters 1, 2

2. Financial performance metrics – financial ratios: Gibson, Chapters 3-9; Subramanyam, Chapters 10, 11

3. Profitability analysis: Gibson, Chapter 8; Subramanyam, Chapter 8

4. Analytical issues in financial accounting: Gibson, Chapter 9; Subramanyam, Chapters 3, 5; Mackenzie, Chapters 8, 11, 20, 22, 23, 35

B. Corporate Finance (25%)

1. Risk and return: Brealey, Chapter 7, 9; Van Horne, Chapter 5

2. Managing financial risk: Brealey, Chapter 26; Van Horne, Chapter 16

3. Financial instruments: Brealey, Chapters 14, 23-25; Van Horne, Chapters 11, 20-22

4. Cost of capital: Brealey, Chapter 9; Van Horne, Chapter 15

5. Managing current assets: Brealey, Chapters 29, 30; Van Horne, Chapters 8-10

6. Raising capital: Brealey, Chapters 23-25; Van Horne, Chapters 19-22

7. Corporate restructuring: Brealey, Chapters 31, 32; Van Horne, Chapter 23

8. International finance: Brealey, Chapter 27; Van Horne, Chapter 24

C. Decision Analysis and Risk Management (25%)

1. Cost/volume/profit analysis: Blocher, Chapter 9; Horngren, Chapter 3

2. Marginal analysis: Blocher, Chapter 11; Horngren, Chapter 11

3. Pricing: Blocher, Chapter 13; Horngren, Chapter 12

4. Risk assessment: Moeller, Chapters 4–8, 16; COSO, Enterprise Risk Management IMA, ERM, Frameworks IMA, ERM, Tools and Techniques

D. Investment Decisions (20%)

1. Capital budgeting process: Brealey, Chapters 5, 6; Van Horne, Chapters 12, 13

2. Discounted cash flow analysis: Brealey, Chapter 6; Van Horne, Chapter 13

3. Payback and discounted payback: Brealey, Chapter 6; Van Horn, Chapter 13

4. Ranking investment projects: Brealey, Chapter 6; Van Horne, Chapter 13

5. Risk analysis in capital investment: Brealey, Chapter 10; Van Horne, Chapter 14

6. Valuation: Brealey, Chapters 3, 4; Van Horne, Chapter 4

E. Professional Ethics (5%)

1. Ethical considerations for the organization U.S. Foreign Corrupt Practices Act IMA's "Values and Ethics: From Inception to Practice"

Practice Exam

The following multiple-choice questions are sample questions you can expect on the CMA test. Please refer to the earlier section on "Parameters to expect on the test" for more details about the CMA test.

Part 1: Financial Planning, Performance and Control

1. The sum of direct labor and factory overhead is termed ___A___.
    a. Sunk costs   *Yup*
    b. Conversion costs *IYup*
    c. Opportunity costs *IYup*
    d. Inventoriable   *IYup*

2. Depreciation of factory equipment would be a cost classified as ___C___.
    a. Direct cost
    b. Indirect cost
    ✶ c. Direct and indirect costs
    d. None of the above

3. Maintenance and repair are what kind of cost?
    a. Variable
    b. Fixed
    c. Semivariable
    (d.) Not a cost

4. Sam is a full time student at a university and needs to decide if she will attend a four week summer school session that costs $250 or take the break and work making $150 per week. What is the opportunity cost?
    a. $250
    b. $600
    c. $350
    d. $850

5. What costs, if any, represent sunk costs?
    a. Depreciation
    b. Rent
    c. Direct materials
    d. Utilities

6. The prime cost formula is:
    a. Direct materials used + direct labor + 50% of sales and administrative expenses
    b. Direct materials used + direct labor
    c. 100% of factory overhead + 50% of selling and administrative expenses
    d. Direct materials used + direct labor + 40% of factory overhead + 60% of selling and administrative expenses

7. An example of discretionary fixed costs would be:
    a. Executive salaries
    b. Rent
    c. Insurance
    d. None of these

8. The cost volume formula showing the relationship between repair costs y and machine hours x came out as y' = $500 + $0.50x where y' is estimated repair costs. What is the slope of the regression line?
    a. x
    b. $0.50
    c. $500
    d. $0.50x

9. _____ is the difference between sales and variable expenses.
    a. Contribution margin
    b. Selling price
    c. Percentage of sales
    d. Volume of activity

10. If the _____ changes, it is necessary to recompute the break-even point for the company as a whole.
    a. Profits
    b. Volume of activity
    c. Sales mix
    d. None of the above

11. There are two ways of expressing target income: as a specific dollar amount and?
    a. Contribution margin
    b. Sales mix
    c. Percentage of sales
    d. Direct materials

12. The following information pertains to the budget of Good Products, Inc. for next year: Sales $50,000,000; Variable Expenses $45,000,000; Fixed Costs $3,000,000. Calculate expected net income for a 15% increase in fixed costs and a 15% decrease in variable expenses.
    a. $8,300,000
    b. $1,700,000
    c. $1,500,000
    d. $(2,500,000)

13. The following information is given for XYZ Corp: Unit sale price $10; Variable Cost per Unit $6; Total Fixed Costs $50,000. Determine the break-even sales in units.
    a. $4
    b. 40%
    c. 17 units
    d. 12,500 units

14. The following data are given for Fun Products Inc which markets multiple products: Sales $65,000; Variable Expenses $39,000; Total Fixed Costs $12,000. Compute the contribution margin ratio.
    a. 17%
    b. 20%
    c. 9%
    d. 40%

15. The following information is given for Now Electronics: Unit Selling Price $250; Variable Cost per Unit $130; Fixed Costs $26,000; Tax Rate 40%. Determine the number of units that should be produced to achieve an after-tax target income of $6000.

    a. 300 units
    b. 500 units
    c. 200 units
    d. 700 units

16. The following information is given for Candy Shop: Fixed Costs $30,000 per period; Variable Costs $5/unit; Selling Price $8/unit. Calculate the sales in units required to produce a net income of 10% of sales.

    a. 13,333 units
    b. 13,636 units
    c. 12,500 units
    d. 15,000 units

17. The contribution approach to pricing or _____ is a method of pricing special orders.

    a. Qualitative
    b. Incremental approach
    c. Variable pricing model
    d. Relevant costs

18. The Big Food Company owns and operates a chain of 125 supermarkets. Budgeted data for the Lakewood store are as follows: Annual Sales $425,000; Annual cost of goods sold and other operating expenses $382,000; Annual building ownership costs (not included previously) $20,000. The company can lease the building to a flower shop for $4,000 per month. Decide whether to continue operating the store or lease it using the total project (or comparative statement) approach.

    a. Close the store and sell the building
    b. Close the store and lease the building
    c. Continue the store as it is
    d. Minimize the store and rent a small section to the flower shop

90

19. Using the data from #18, decide whether to continue operating the store or lease it using the incremental (or relevant cost) approach.

    a. Close the store

    b. Close the store and lease the building

    c. Continue the store as it is

    d. Minimize the store and rent a small section to the flower shop

20. Using the data from #18, decide whether to continue operating the store or lease it using the opportunity cost approach.

    a. Difference in favor of closing the store and sell the building

    b. Difference in favor of closing the store and lease the building

    c. Difference in favor of continuing the store as it is

    d. Difference in favor of minimizing the store and rent a small section to the flower shop

21. Trunk Company manufactures part no. 1700 for use in its production cycle. The costs per unit for a 5,000 unit quantity follows: Direct materials $2; Direct labor $12; Variable overhead $5; Fixed overhead applied $7; Total costs $26. ABC Company has offered to sell 5,000 units of part no. 1700 for $27 per unit. If Truck accepts the offer, some of the facilities currently used to make part no. 1700 could be used to help make part no. 1211. This would save $40,000 in relevant costs in the manufacture of part no. 1211 and $3 per unit of the fixed overhead applied to part no. 1700 would be totally eliminated. By what amount would net relevant costs be increased or decreased if Truck accepts ABC's offer?

    a. $35,000 decrease

    b. $20,000 decrease

    c. $15,000 decrease

    d. $5,000 increase

22. Ray Corporation manufactures batons. Ray can manufacture 300,000 batons a year at a variable cost of $750,000 and a fixed cost of $450,000. Based on Ray's predictions, 240,000 batons will be sold at a regular price of $5 each. In addition, a special order was placed for 60,000 batons to be sold at a 40% discount off the regular price. By what amount would income be increased or decreased as a result of the special order?
    a. $60,000 decrease
    b. $30,000 increase
    c. $36,000 increase
    d. $180,000 increase

23. Blue Jay Company needs 20,000 units of a certain part to use in its production cycle. The following information is available: Direct materials $4; Direct labor $16; Variable overhead $8; Fixed overhead $10; Total costs to make the part $38; Cost to buy the part from Orin Co $36. If Blue Jay buys the part from Orin instead of making it, Blue Jay could not use the released facilities in another manufacturing activity. Sixty percent of the fixed overhead applied will continue, regardless of what decision is made. In deciding whether to make or buy the part, the total relevant costs to make the part are:
    a. $560,000
    b. $640,000
    c. $720,000
    d. $760,000

24. The Nevada Company manufactures part no. 498 for use in its production cycle. The cost per unit for 20,000 units of part no. 498 are as follows: Direct materials $ 6; Direct labor $ 30; Variable overhead $ 12; Fixed overhead applied $ 16; Total costs $64. The Fray Company has offered to sell 20,000 units of part no. 498 to Nevada for $60 per unit. Nevada will make the decision to buy the part from Fray if there is a $25,000 savings for Nevada. If Nevada accepts Fray's offer, $9 per unit of fixed overhead applied will be eliminated. In addition, Nevada has determined that the release of the facilities could be used to save relevant costs of manufacturing part no. 575. In order to have savings of $25,000, the amount of relevant costs that would be saved using the released facilities in the manufacture of part no. 575 would have to be: (AICPA, adopted)
    a. $80,000
    b. $85,000
    c. $125,000
    d. $140,000

25. _____ is so named because budgeting starts from scratch.
    a. Zero-based budgeting
    b. Production budgeting
    c. Inventory budgeting
    d. Budgeted balance sheet

26. The following data pertain to the budget of Smart Industries: Beginning inventory 30,000 units; Planned sales $100,000; Desired ending inventory 20,000 units. Compute the production volume required.
    a. 45,000 units
    b. 75,000 units
    c. 85,000 units
    d. 90,000 units

27. The following data pertain to the budget of Stuff Industries: Beginning inventory 10,000 units; Planned sales $50,000; Desired ending inventory 5,000 units. Compute the production volume required.
    a. 45,000 units
    b. 75,000 units
    c. 85,000 units
    d. 90,000 units

28. (Use this data for questions 28 to 33) The Fray Company marks up all merchandise at 25% of gross purchase price. All purchases are made on account with terms of 1/10, net/60. Purchase discounts, which are recorded as miscellaneous income, are always taken. Normally, 60% of each month's purchases are paid in the month of the purchase, while the other 40% are paid in the first 10 days of the first month after purchase. Inventories of merchandise at the end of each month are kept at 30% of the next month's projected costs of goods sold. Terms for sales on account are 2/10 and net/30. Cash sales are not subject to discount. 50% of each month's sales on account are collected during the month of the sale, 45% are collected in the succeeding month and the remained is usually uncollected. 70% of the collections in the month are subject to discount while 10% are subject to discount in the preceding month. Projected sales data for selected months follow: December: Sales on Account – Gross $1,900,000; Cash Sales $400,000; Total Sales $2,300,000 January: Sales on Account – Gross $1,500,000; Cash Sales $250,000; Total Sales $1,750,000 February: Sales on Account – Gross $1,700,000; Cash Sales $350,000; Total Sales $2,050,000 March: Sales on Account – Gross $1,600,000; Cash Sales $300,000; Total Sales $1,900,000. Projected gross purchases for January are:
    a. $1,400,000
    b. $1,470,000
    c. $1,472,000
    d. $1,248,000

29. Using data from question 28, projected inventory at the end of December is:
    a. $420,000
    b. $441,600
    c. $552,000
    d. $393,750

30. Using data from question 28, projected payments to suppliers during February are:
    a. $1,551,200
    b. $1,535,688
    c. $1,528,560
    d. $1,509,552

31. Using data from question 28, projected sales discounts to be taken by customers making remittances during February are:
    a. $5,250
    b. $15,925
    c. $30,500
    d. None of the above

32. Using data from question 28, projected total collections from customers during February are:
    a. $1,875,000
    b. $1,861,750
    c. $1,511,750
    d. 1,188,100

33. _____ is called profitability accounting and activity accounting.
    a. Responsibility accounting
    b. Cost accounting
    c. Revenue accounting
    d. Inventory accounting

34. The contribution approach to _____ (or performance evaluation) is widely used for profitability analysis of various segments of an organization.
    a. Investment centers
    b. Cost allocation
    c. Production budgeting
    d. Responsibility accounting

35. _____ are those costs that are directly influenced by a manager within a given time span.
    a. Controllable costs
    b. Fixed costs
    c. Production costs
    d. Insurance costs

36. A variance is said to be _____ if the actual price or the actual quantity exceeds the standard price or the standard quantity.
    a. High
    b. Low
    c. Unfavorable
    d. Favorable

37. Opportunity costs:
    a. Do not appear on formal accounting statements.
    b. Do not require dollar outlays.
    c. Both of the above
    d. None of the above

38. Assume that two products are manufactured from a joint process. Product B has additional revenue of $12,000 after additional processing costs of $9,000 and allocate joint costs of $25,000. It should be:
    a. Sold at the split-off point
    b. Processed further
    c. Both of the above
    d. None of the above

39. The sales budget can be classified as:
    a. A capital budget
    b. An operating budget
    c. A master budget
    d. A financial budget

40. In preparing a merchandise purchase budget during a selected month, one must have information on:
    a. The beginning inventory
    b. The desired ending inventory
    c. The amount of materials required for production
    d. All of the above

41. If a cost can be allocated to certain segments of an organization, it should be:
    a. Excluded from the segmented income statement
    b. Included in it
    c. Included in it but not allocated
    d. None of the above

42. A cost that can be eliminated if a particular division is discounted is called:
    a. An opportunity cost
    b. An incremental cost
    c. A variable cost
    d. An avoidable cost

43. A cash budget consists of a:
    a. Cash receipts section
    b. Cash disbursements section
    c. Financing section
    d. All of the above

44. The number of units to be produced is equal to planned sales in units:
    a. + the desired ending inventory – the beginning inventory of finished goods
    b. + the beginning inventory – the desired ending inventory of finished goods
    c. Neither of the above
    d. Both a and b

45. The Copper Company has limited capacity in terms of the number of labor hours available. To maximize the profit of the company, it should concentrate on a product with the highest:
    a. Total sales
    b. Contribution margin per machine hour
    c. Contribution margin per unit of output
    d. None of the above

46. In designing a responsibility system, one should keep in mind a certain characteristic of each cost. This characteristic is:
    a. The degree of cost controllability by the manager
    b. How the cost behaves with respect to volume
    c. The accuracy of cost allocation
    d. All of the above

47. A(n) _____ has control over both profits and investment.
    a. Revenue center
    b. Investment center
    c. Production center
    d. None of the above

48. Decentralization is the delegation of _____ to individual divisions of an organization.
    a. Goal congruence
    b. Performance evaluation
    c. Decision making
    d. Turnover

49. Operating income divided by sales is referred to as _____.
    a. Revenue
    b. Margin
    c. Residual income
    d. Cost

50. _____ less a minimum rate of return on operating assets is referred to as residual income (RI).
    a. Operating income
    b. Investment income
    c. Return on investment
    d. Market price

51. Travis Corp obtains average cash receipts of $200,000 per day. It usually takes 5 days from the time a check is mailed to its availability for use. The amount tied up in the delay is:
    a. $200,000
    b. $500,000
    c. $1,000,000
    d. None of the above

52. The opportunity cost of not taking a discount when the terms are 3/15, net/60 is:
    a. 30%
    b. 17.5%
    c. 14.3%
    d. 24.7%

53. Excess cash that will be needed in the near future should be temporarily invested in _____ securities.
    a. Marketable ✓
    b. Banking ✓
    c. Both a and b
    d. None of the above

54. One way to defer a cash payment is by the use of a(n) _____, because the bank must first secure approval from the company before the instrument is paid.
    a. Note
    b. Draft
    c. Deposit
    d. Balance

55. The terms of a $1,000 sale are 3/20, net/40. If collection is received in 14 days, that amount received is $_____.
    a. $1,000
    b. $800
    c. $970
    d. $790

56. On a typical day, WRD Company write checks totaling $3,000. These checks clear in 7 days. At the same time, the company receives $1,700. The cash is available in 2 days on average. Calculate the disbursement float.
    a. $9,000
    b. $21,000
    c. $1,700
    d. $3,400

57. Using data from question 56, calculate the collection float.
    a. $1,700
    b. $3,400
    c. -$1,700
    d. -$3,400

58. Using data from question 56, calculate the net float.
    a. $17,600
    b. $14,500
    c. $20,700
    d. $19,600

59. The terms of sale is 3/20, net/45, May 1 dating. What is the last date the company may pay in order to receive a discount?
    a. May 31
    b. June 15
    c. May 20
    d. May 15

60. Rock Corporation sells on terms of net/90. Their accounts receivable are on average 20 days past due. If annual credit sales are $800,000, what is the company's average investment in accounts receivable?
    a. $200,000
    b. $244,444
    c. $400,000
    d. $444,444

61. Mason Corporation purchases 3,000 units of a raw material at a list price of $5 each. The supplier offers a quantity discount of 4%. What is the material cost on the item?
    a. $15,000
    b. $600
    c. $14,400
    d. None of the above

62. Sally Corp uses 8,500 units per year. Each order is for 200 units. The cost per order is $13. What is the total ordering cost for the year?
    a. $8,500.50
    b. $200.25
    c. $1,300.75
    d. $552.50

63. Use this data for questions 63-67. All U Need Appliance sells an average of 160 units per month. Each order the store places is for 300 units. The cost per unit is $5. The cost per order is $12. Carrying cost is $0.15 per dollar invested per year. The rate of return is 18%. The tax rate is 46%. What is the investment in average inventory?
    a. $600
    b. $750
    c. $950
    d. $300

64. Using data from question 63, what is the annual ordering cost?
    a. $76.80
    b. $82.70
    c. $43.85
    d. None of the above

65. Using data from question 63, what is the annual holding cost?
    a. $750.25
    b. $112.50
    c. $97.75
    d. $325.50

66. Using data from question 63, what is the opportunity cost of holding inventory?
    a. $300
    b. $160
    c. $135
    d. $275

67. Using data from question 63, what is the total cost of the inventory excluding the purchase price?
    a. $76.80
    b. $112.50
    c. $135
    d. $237.22

68. _____ loans are those in which the loan is paid as soon as the financed assets realize cash.
    a. Unsecured
    b. Commercial
    c. Bankers' acceptance
    d. Self-liquidating

69. A(n) _____ refers to the deposit, which does not earn interest, that a company must maintain at the bank as collateral for a loan.
    a. Installment
    b. Credit rating
    c. Compensating balance
    d. Bankers' acceptance

70. The outright sale of accounts receivable to a third party is __B__.
    a. Trade credit
    b. Factoring
    c. Assignment
    d. Installment

71. In case of inventory financing, a(n) __A__ lien applies to the aggregate inventory rather than the components.
    a. Floating (blanket)
    b. Mechanic's
    c. Tax
    d. None of the above

72. Phillip Corporation purchases $750 per day from suppliers on terms of net/30. Determine the accounts payable balance.
    a. $750
    b. $225
    c. $10,750
    d. $22,500

73. Kym Corp. borrows $150,000 from a bank. A 10% compensating balance is required. What is the amount of the compensating balance?
    a. $15,000
    b. $10,000
    c. $7,500
    d. $5,000

74. Carl Company borrows $500,000 form a bank and is required to maintain a 15% compensating balance. In addition, Carl has an unused line of credit of $200,000 with a required 11% compensating balance. What is the total required compensating balance the firm must maintain?
    a. $50,000
    b. $20,000
    c. $97,000
    d. $100,000

75. Jones Corporation borrows $70,000 at 19% annual interest. Principal and interest are due in one year. What is the effective interest rate?
    a. 10%
    b. 19%
    c. 23%
    d. 5%

Part 2: Financial Decision Making

1. The three major categories of the statement of cash flows are cash flows associated with _____ activities, investing activities and financing activities.
   a. Operating
   b. Production
   c. Sales and administration
   d. None of the above

2. The return on equity is the return on total assets multiplied by the _____.
   a. Yield
   b. Liabilities
   c. Equity multiplier
   d. Net income

3. Depreciating expense is one of the items that must be added back to net income to determine the cash flows from _____ activities.
   a. Production
   b. Sales and administration
   c. Financing
   d. Operating

4. There are two basic approaches to cost accounting and accumulation, and they are _____ and process costing.
   a. Job-order costing
   b. Overhead costing
   c. Production costing
   d. None of the above

5. With _____, the focus is to apply costs to specific jobs, which may consist of either a single physical unit or a few like units.
   a. Process costing
   b. Job-order costing
   c. Both a and b
   d. None of the above

6. Under process costing, accounting data are accumulated by the _____ and averaged over all of the production that occurred in the department.
   a. Production department
   b. Cost center
   c. Both a and b
   d. None of the above

7. In order for job costs to be available on a timely basis, it is customary to apply factory overhead by using a _____.
   a. Cost driver
   b. Machine hour
   c. Unit measurement
   d. Predetermined factory overhead rate

8. Overhead is applied to jobs using a(n) _____ multiplied by actual cost driver usage.
   a. Unit measurement
   b. Predetermined factory overhead rate
   c. Both a and b
   d. None of the above

9. Process costing is appropriate for companies that produce a continuous mass of _____ through a series of operations or processes.
   a. Like units
   b. Direct materials
   c. Direct labor
   d. Variable overhead

10. In process costing, 100 units that are 60% completed are the equivalent of completed how many units in terms of conversion costs?
    a. 40
    b. 60
    c. 80
    d. 75

11. _____ are those that have a relatively significant sales value.
    ✗ a. By-products
    ✗ b. Split-points
    ✗ c. Joint products
      d. None of the above

12. _____ are those whose sales value is relatively minor in comparison with the value of the main product.
    (a) By-products
     b. Split-points
     c. Joint products
     d. None of the above

13. Activity based accounting (ABC) traces costs to _____ and then products.
     a. Costs
     b. Activities
    ✗ c. Drivers
     d. Demand

14. ABC is not an alternative costing system to _____ costing or process costing.
     a. Job
     b. Production
     c. Financial
     d. Overhead

15. Just-in-time (JIT) manufacturing is a _____, rather than the traditional "push" approach.
    ✗ a. Drag
    ✗ b. Drop
    ✗ c. Demand-pull
    ✗ d. Demand-withhold

16. The primary goal of JIT is to reduce _____ to insignificant or zero levels.
     a. Production
     b. Sales
     c. Yield
    (d) Inventory

17. JIT cannot be implemented without a commitment to _____.
    a. Production
    ✗ b. Total quality control (TQC)
    c. Sales
    d. None of the above

18. The cost accounting system of a company adopting JIT will be quite simple compared to _____.
    ✗ a. Job-order costing
    ✗ b. Process costing
    c. Both a and b
    d. None of the above

19. _____ is a zero defects approach.

    a. Total quality control (TQC)
    b. Total quality management (TQM)
    c. Both a and b
    d. None of the above

20. Quality costs are classified in to three broad categories: prevention, appraisal and _____ costs.
    a. Failure
    b. Yield
    c. Processing
    d. Sales

21. Quality experts say that the optimal quality level should be about ___ of sales.
    a. 10%
    b. 20%
    c. 5.5%
    d. 2.5%

22. One of the most important aspects of cost accounting is _____ for inventory valuation and income determination.
    a. Financial accounting
    b. Coordination
    c. Cost accumulation
    d. None of the above

23. Historical costs that cannot be recovered by any decision made now or in the future are called _____.
    a. Conversion costs
    b. Sunk costs
    c. Opportunity costs
    d. Production costs

24. The beginning finished goods inventory plus the _____, minus the ending finished goods inventory equals the cost of goods sold for a manufacturer.
    a. Factory overhead
    b. Conversion cost
    c. Standard cost
    d. Cost of goods manufactured

25. Payroll fringe benefits are generally classified as _____.
    a. Factory overhead
    b. Production costs
    c. Both a and b
    d. None of the above

26. _____ encourages investment in projects that would otherwise be rejected under return on investment (ROI).
    a. Investment income
    b. Market price
    c. Operating income
    d. Residual income (RI)

27. The harmonizing of manager's goals with the organization's goals is called _____.
    a. Flow chart organization
    b. Goal congruence
    c. Performance review
    d. Team training

28. A transfer price based on _____ will lead to optimal economic decision under the conditions of the existence of competitive market price and independence of divisions.
    a. Market price
    b. Industry standard
    c. Indexing
    d. Sales

29. Many firms base transfer prices on ____, since they are easy to understand and convenient to use.
    a. Sales
    b. Cost
    c. Market price
    d. Industry standard

30. Transfer prices based on full cost are appropriate if top management treats the divisions like ____.
    a. Departments
    b. Individual companies
    c. Cost centers
    d. None of the above

31. ADC, a division of ABC Manufacturing, has assets of $225,000and an operating income of $55,000. What is the division's ROI?
    a. 37.05%
    b. 24.44%
    c. 15.75%
    d. 10.36%

32. Using data from question 56, if the minimum rate of return is 12%, what is the division's residual income?
    a. $28,000
    b. $34,000
    c. $17,000
    d. $42,000

33. The following data is given for the Florida division for 201X: ROI 25%; Sales $1,200,000; Margin 10%; Minimum required rate of return 18%. Compute the division's operating assets.
    a. $1,200,000
    b. $500,000
    c. $480,000
    d. None of the above

34. Using data from question 58, compute the division's residual income (RI).
    a. $120,000
    b. $86,400
    c. $30,000
    d. $33,600

35. The NVP method and the IRR method are called _____ methods.
    a. Financial accounting
    b. Discounted cash flow (DCF)
    c. Cost accounting
    d. None of the above

36. _____ is the process of making long-term decisions.
    a. Capital budgeting
    b. Investment budgeting
    c. Cost budgeting
    d. Production budgeting

37. Accounting rate of return does not recognize __C__.
   a. Payback period
   b. Cost allocation
   c. Time value of money
   d. None of the above

38. Accept the investment if its IRR exceeds __A__.
   a. The cost of capital
   b. Initial investment
   c. ROI
   d. All of the above

39. IRR is difficult to compute when the cash flows are __d__.
   a. Balanced
   b. Even
   c. Reconciled
   d. Not even

40. __C__ is obtained by multiplying the depreciation deduction by the income tax rate.
   a. IRR
   b. ROI
   c. Tax shield
   d. None of the above

41. Immediate disposal of the old machine usually results in __b__ that is fully deductible from current income for tax purposes.
   a. A gain
   b. A loss
   c. A reimbursement
   d. None of the above

42. __D__ are values of decision variables that satisfy all the restrictions simultaneously.
   a. Objective functions
   b. Constraints
   c. Non-negatives
   d. Feasible solutions

43. One way of computing the safety stock size is to multiply the difference between
_____ and average lead time.
    a. Demand
    b. Constraints
    c. Maximum usage
    d. Lead time

44. In computing the safety stock, the decision maker tries to balance off the costs of
____ and the costs of carrying inventory.
    a. Stockouts (or shortage)
    b. Lead time
    c. Loss
    d. None of the above

45. The following information relates to the Karry Company: Units required per year
30,000; Cost of placing an order $400; Unit carrying cost per year $600. Assuming
that the units will be required evenly throughout the year, what is the economic
order quantity?
    a. 400
    b. 600
    c. 200
    d. 100

46. _D_ is the ability for a company to meet its current liabilities out of current assets.
    a. Yield
    b. Equity
    c. Earnings
    d. Liquidity

47. The current ratio is equal to __a__ divided by current liabilities.
    a. Current assets
    b. Accounts receivables
    c. Payout
    d. Inventory

48. _____ is included in computing the current ratio but not the quick ratio.
    a. Equity
    b. Inventory
    c. Net income
    d. None of the above

49. The accounts receivable turnover is equal to _____ divided by average accounts receivable.
    a. Net income
    b. Earnings
    c. Yield
    d. Net credit sales

50. Financial statement analysis should combine _____ and industry comparisons.
    a. Net credit sales
    b. Earnings
    c. Liabilities
    d. Trend analysis

51. Still Water Corporation is deciding which bank to borrow from on a 1-year basis. Bank A charges an 18% interest rate payable at maturity. Bank B charges 17% interest rate on a discount basis. Which loan is cheaper?
    a. Bank A
    b. Bank B
    c. Both a and b
    d. Neither a or b

52. Use this data for questions 52-54. Wise Guy Company borrows $70,000 payable in 12 monthly installments. The interest rate is 15%. What is the average loan balance?
    a. $70,000
    b. $35,000
    c. $95,000
    d. None of the above

53. Using data from question 52, what is the effective interest rate?

    a. 15%

    b. 45%

    c. 30%

    d. 20%

54. Using data from question 52, except that the loan in on a discount basis. What is the average loan balance?

    a. $29,750

    b. $59,500

    c. $35,000

    d. $70,000

55. Using data from question 54, what is the effective interest rate?

    a. 15%

    b. 35.3%

    c. 22.4%

    d. None of the above

56. Ned Company issues $800,000 of commercial paper every 3 months at a 16% rate. Each issuance involves a placement cost of $2,000. What is the annual percentage cost of the commercial paper?

    a. 10%

    b. 20%

    c. 17%

    d. 23%

57. The Stevenson Company expects it will need $600,000 cash for March 20X2. Possible means of financing are: (a.) Establish a 1-year credit line for $600,000. The bank requires a 2% commitment fee. The interest rate is 21% and the funds are needed for 30 days. (b.) Fail to take a 2/10, net/40 discount on a $600,000 credit purchase. (c.) Issue $600,000, 20% commercial paper for 30 days. Which financing strategy should be selected?

    a. The credit line

    b. No discount

    c. Commercial paper

    d. None of the above

58. Peter Company is contemplating factoring its accounts receivable. The factor will require $250,000 of the company's accounts receivable every 2 months. An advance of 75% is given by the factor on receivables at an annual charge of 18%. There is a 2% factor fee associated with receivables purchased. What is the cost of the factoring arrangement?

    a. $30,000

    b. $63,750

    c. $33,750

    d. $70,000

59. _____ results in the maximum possible future value at the end of n periods for a given rate of interest.

    a. Annual percentage rate

    b. Intrayear compounding

    c. Straight amortization

    d. Continuous compounding

60. The _____ is the annual deposit (or payment) of an amount that is necessary to accumulate a specified future sum.

    a. Sinking fund

    b. Perpetuity

    c. Straight amortization

    d. Continuous compounding

61. ___D___ refers to the variability of expected return (or earnings) associated with a given investment.

    a. Probability

    b. Variation

    c. Distribution

    (d.) Risk

62. Portfolio risk can be reduced by ___A___.

    (a.) Diversification

    b. Probability

    c. Business risk

    d. Capital gain

63. The valuation process involves finding the _____ of an asset's expected future cash flows using the investor's required rate of return.
   a. Risk
   b. Present value
   c. Diversification
   d. Capital gain

64. The one-period return on stock investment is dividends plus _____, divided by the beginning price.
   a. Capital gain
   b. Present value
   c. Risk
   d. Probability

65. Unlike the capital asset pricing model (CAPM), the _____ includes any number of risk factors.
   a. Security market line (SML) ✓
   (b) Arbitrage pricing model (APM) ✓
   c. Both a and b
   d. Neither a or b

66. Assume that the risk-free rate of return is 8%, the required rate of return on the market is 13% and the stock X has a beta coefficient of 1.5. What is stock X's rate of return?
   a. 16.5%
   b. 18%
   c. 15.5%
   d. 19%

67. Nancy Czech is considering the purchase of stock X at the beginning of the year. The dividend at year-end is expected to be $3.25 and the market price by the end of the year is expected to be $25. If she requires a rate of return of 12%, what is the value of the stock?
   a. $22.33
   b. $25.23
   c. $28.25
   d. $21.75

68. Accounting rate of return does not recognize the time value of __C__.
    a. Costs
    b. Revenue
    c. Money
    d. Stocks

69. __D__ is used widely in ranking the investments competing for limited funds.
    a. Profitability index
    b. Benefit/cost ratio
    c. Cost of capital
    d. Both a and b are the same thing

70. __D__ is taken in the year in which an asset is first placed in to service.
    a. Investment tax credit (ITC)
    b. A loss
    c. Depreciation
    d. All of the above

71. The rate of return required for a company's security is equal to the __A__ plus a risk premium.
    a. Risk-free rate
    b. Opportunity cost
    c. Corporate risk
    d. None of the above

72. Relative risk is measured by __D__.
    a. Revenues
    b. Production
    c. Sensitivity analysis
    d. Coefficient of variation

73. Beta is an index of __D__ risk.
    a. Systematic
    b. Non-controllable
    c. Non-diversifiable
    d. All of the above

74. The ___A___ is found by dividing the annual preferred stock dividend by the net proceeds from sale.
    a. Cost of preferred stock
    b. Cost of common stock
    c. Cost of valuation
    d. None of the above

75. The cost of new common stock is higher than the cost of common because of ___C___ involved in its sale.
    a. Market value
    b. Book value
    c. Flotation costs
    d. Margins